Lieber's Code and the Law of War

Lieber's Code and the Law of War

Richard Shelly Hartigan

Precedent
Chicago
1983

International Standard Book Number: 0-913750-25-5

Library of Congress Catalog Card Number: 82-62843

 Published by Precedent Publishing, Inc., 520 North Michigan Avenue, Chicago, IL 60611.

Printed in the United States of America.

Contents

Preface

Francis Lieber influenced the minds and practices of lawyers, scholars and governments in Europe and America with what he himself termed "a little pamphlet" that did not even bear his name formally as its principal author.

Lieber's work has not been forgotten. There exists an extensive bibliography on his life, his political philosophy, and his influence. Yet his two most important works are largely inaccessible to any but a very narrow academic community. He deserves a much wider audience. This book restores to general availability the two most mature and relevant of Lieber's works.

I have added to the texts a number of letters that place Lieber in the context of the American Civil War, which provoked his civilizing labor. The reader who wishes a more complete view of his life and times will find them most adequately treated by authors cited in my introduction and bibliography.

I gratefully acknowledge the assistance of my research associates Sheli Lulkin and Terry Gough. My son Patrick and my daughter Jennifer helped me in many ways, at various stages. Ms. Harriet McLoone of the Huntington Library gave prompt and accurate responses to my research needs. Finally I must also thank the Earhart Foundation for its support, and in particular, Mr. Antony Sullivan.

Richard Shelly Hartigan
Chicago, 1982

Introduction: Francis Lieber and the Law of War

by Richard Shelly Hartigan

> If our Society, at once national and international, were about to choose a patron saint, and the roll were to be called, my voice for one would answer "Francis Lieber."
>
> Elihu Root, "Presidential Address"
> American Society of International Law
> April 24, 1913

Fifty years to the day before the distinguished Elihu Root affirmed his preference for a patron saint, when the United States of America was in the throes of a civil war, the War Department published a landmark order:

> General Orders, War Dept., Adjt. General's Office
> No. 100. Washington, April 24, 1863.
>
> The following instructions for the government of armies of the United States in the field, prepared by Francis Lieber, LL. D., and revised by a board of officers of which Maj. Gen. E. A. Hitchcock is president, having been approved by the President of the United States, he commands that they be published for the information of all concerned.
>
> By order of the Secretary of War:
> E. D. Townsend,
> Assistant Adjutant-General[1]

This document was to have a profound effect on the international law of land warfare. The governments of Prussia, France and Great Britain copied it. The Hague and Geneva Conventions were indebted directly to it. Though buried in voluminous United States government publications, the "General Orders, no. 100" remains a benchmark for the conduct of an army toward an enemy army and population. It will be cited hereafter simply as Lieber's Code.

The Code was the first instance in western history in which the government of a sovereign nation established formal guidelines for its army's conduct toward its enemies. Previously, kingdoms, empires, and nation states had decreed how their armies should be internally disciplined, while international law theorists had written treatises on how belligerent states should treat each other's armies, prisoners and civilian populations; but never before had a government set down in clear, explicit, formal terms not only the rights and obligations of its own army, but of its enemy's army and civil population as well.

Dr. Francis Lieber was a highly regarded German immigrant law professor at the then Columbia College in New York. Among his admirers was Henry Wager Halleck, General-in-Chief of the Union Armies, himself a student and author in the field of international law.[2] On August 6, 1862, Halleck wrote to Lieber to request his assistance in defining guerrilla warfare.

> My Dear Doctor: Having heard that you have given much attention to the usages and customs of war as practiced in the present age, and especially to the matter of guerrilla war, I hope you may find it convenient to give to the public your views on that subject. The rebel authorities claim the right to send men, in the garb of peaceful citizens, to waylay and attack our troops, to burn bridges and houses and to destroy property and persons within our lines. They demand that such persons be treated as ordinary belligerents, and that when captured they have extended to them the same rights as other prisoners of war; they also threaten that if such persons be punished as marauders and spies they will retaliate by executing our prisoners of war in their possession. I particularly request your views on these questions.[3]

Lieber's lengthy reply constituted an essay on the definition and nature of guerrilla war and the status and rights of the participants, with a compendium of historical examples. The essay remains today as relevant and sound in most of its definitions as when it was written.

But Lieber had a grander project in mind. In August 1861, he had written:

> I desire to write a little book on the Law and Usages of War, affecting the combatants, some 200 pages 12 mo., but nothing of the sort having ever been written, so far as I know, it would re-

> quire a good deal of hunting up, and God has denied me the two delectable things, a saddle horse and an amanuensis. Otherwise I would try to write something which Congress might feel inclined to recommend to the Army.[4]

It would be two years before his project was fulfilled as "General Orders, no. 100." His initial public anonymity as its principal author has been redressed by the later influence of the Code.

i

Military commanders from time immemorial had set down rules and regulations to discipline their troops. From the Pharaohs on, commanders directed the strategy, tactics, and camp discipline of the often unruly hosts of soldiers under their command. They had one aim: to create an efficient fighting force. Centurions, camp-followers and cooks were all expected to perform their services according to mandate and in light of the best interests of the armed force and the fighting soldiery. Modern commanders have exemplified the same passion for military discipline to produce an effective combat machine.

St. Augustine, writing in the fifth century twilight of the Roman Empire, declared in his *City of God* that a Christian might engage without sin in a "just war," which he then proceeded to define. In succeeding centuries Christian theologians and secular jurists redefined and elaborated Augustine's views. The result was a body of theoretical treatises dealing with just war in its incidence, conduct and resolution. A high point was reached in the sixteenth and seventeenth centuries with the writing of Francisco de Vitoria and Hugo Grotius. Their works are acknowledged as the analytical bases of the contemporary international law of land warfare. They were followed by such theorists as Vattel and Bynkershoek. Their analyses, derived from Roman *jus gentium* (law of peoples) and containing enough historical examples to fill an encyclopaedia, were impressive. Yet, although addressed to the problems of their day, they generally remained the private counsel of scholars and had little impact on political and military decisions. Although Vitoria's ideas of justice toward the New

World Indians under Spanish control did have some indirect policy effect in the sixteenth century, this was the exception rather than the rule. By the nineteenth century two parallel traditions of the warrior's code had developed among the military and civilians, sometimes overlapping, but usually separate.[5]

Through the centuries the civil theorists evolved a set of dicta based on natural law theory, religious and secular, combined it with their view of custom, practice and law, and pronounced a law of nations which ought to be binding on all societies. To a degree, and at times, their admonitions that "just war" should be conducted justly, that noncombatants should be spared outrageous violence, and that war should only serve a political purpose were coincidentally reflected in the policy of their times. Thus the Swiss jurist, Emrich von Vattel, could write in the middle of the eighteenth century that even though women, children, feeble old men and the sick were among the enemy, "the belligerent has no right to maltreat . . . them, much less to put them to death. There is today no Nation in any degree civilized which does not observe this rule of justice and humanity."[6] If violations of immunity did occur, he enjoined officers to punish those of their men who were guilty. But the eighteenth century was an exceptional period and Vattel's optimistic reflection on the practice of civilized nations, though generally or partly correct, was also premature. Subsequent violations of the prisoners and civilian populations in European and American warfare would prove Vattel to have been too sanguine.

While the theorists of international law were developing a body of rules to govern warfare, the practitioners of conflict were largely moved by the motives of military necessity and pursued the means necessary to obtain the victory. Machiavelli and Clausewitz nicely summed up military necessity, the latter stating in his *On War*, "War therefore is an act of violence intended to compel our opponent to fulfill our will."[7] This statement, taken out of context, gives the impression that the nineteenth century Prussian theoretician of war was a fanatic who raised war to the level of an end in itself. Nothing could be further from the truth, but the statement does convey the sense of grim determination contained in the notion of military necessity. Under the dual auspices of military necessity and national self-interest, the code of the military commander was simple: maintain a disciplined fighting force in order to achieve military victory. His purposes had little in common with the scholarly ideas and ideals of theorists like Grotius and Vattel.

This does not mean that commanders and their soldiers regularly acted viciously toward their enemy and its civilian population. By the nineteenth century well disciplined national armies often showed an amazing forebearance toward the enemy, both on and off the battlefield. Yet restraint did not stem from a conscious articulation of principles of international law so much as from a kind of soldier's honor not unlike the medieval chivalric code of the fair fight. The theories of international legal writers had not substantially permeated the military and political policies of nations.

To remedy this gap between theory and practice, a practical guide was needed which would briefly describe for commanders in the field the rights and obligations of belligerents as custom and theory had developed them. Then political and military policy could be expected to conform to the theoretical law of nations. This was the synthesis that the Lieber Code proposed.

ii

Lieber was born in Berlin at the turn of the nineteenth century and lived through its most turbulent years in Europe and America.[8] Before emigrating to the United States in 1827 he had already enjoyed a full life. He fought under Blücher at Waterloo, was seriously wounded at the battle of Namur, was imprisoned for expressing anti-state sentiments in Prussia, received a Doctor of Philosophy degree in 1820 from the University of Jena, and fought in the Greek War of Independence. He left Greece for Rome and became a tutor to the family of Georg Niebuhr, the Prussian ambassador and historian, whose friendship was to be of great help after Niebuhr's return to Prussia when he was imprisoned. Niebuhr secured his release and Lieber moved to England, where he stayed for a year before emigrating to Boston in 1827.[9] He became head of the Boston Gymnasium, editor of the *Encyclopaedia Americana*, and in 1835 accepted the Chair of History and Political Economy at South Carolina College, where he taught for twenty-two years. In 1857 he became Professor of Modern History, Political Science and International, Civil and Common Law at Columbia College in New York, a post which he held until his death twenty-five years later. After the Civil War, he worked on the Confederate archives for the War Department and as an umpire under the Mexican Claims Commission.

Lieber's life and career seem somewhat ambivalent. He was a life-long foe of slavery, but muted his feelings during his lengthy stay at South Carolina College. He coined the term "publicist" to describe himself, but he was a scholar and as such his works, especially *Political Ethics* (1838) and *Civil Liberty and Self Government* (1853), earned him a well-deserved reputation. In Europe he had been vehemently active against authoritarianism; he became an ardent nationalist spokesman and apologist for a strong central government in America. One of his biographers describes him as a nineteenth century liberal while another writes of him as an American conservative.[10] In fact, he was both liberal and conservative, in the sense of being passionately committed to individual liberty on the one hand and communal stability on the other. Lieber's dual commitment explains his desire to see his adopted country at peace, unified, with all its members free; like many citizens, he set aside the first of these goals to secure the latter two.

iii

On March 4, 1863, Lieber wrote to General Halleck that "either the North simply and plainly conquers the South . . . or the North must submit in abject, vile serfdom. We must conquer the South not for a crown, as a province, but for the *country* and the *National* Constitution."[11] Lieber had mixed personal and ideological motives during the Civil War. His three sons were engaged in the fighting on both sides. Hamilton lost an arm as a Union soldier at the battle of Fort Donelson. Norman, also a Union soldier, fought against his Confederate brother, Oscar, at the battle of Williamsburg where Oscar died from his wounds, cursing his father and the Northern cause. Throughout his personal tragedy, Lieber maintained a steadfast commitment to the twin goals of preserving the Union and freeing the slaves. To accomplish these civilized ends by civilized means he felt it was essential to bring order and discipline to the Union armies and to define precisely the status of the enemy troops and population.

Lieber's concern for army discipline was provoked by the fact that both the Union and Confederate armies were manned by untrained volunteers and conscripts and largely commanded by politically appointed officers whose military and legal training rarely, if at all, rose above the level of their troops. Complicating this situation was the question of belligerent status. Were the Confederates rebels and therefore traitors, or were they, as they claimed, secessionists who could validly enjoy the belligerent rights of a sovereign state at war under international law?

Here some distinctions must be made between kinds of violence against the state authority from within the community. A coup d'état forces a sudden change in governmental leadership: one regime is supplanted by another, with violence usually limited to the leadership and would-be leaders of the existing state, and their close adherents. Rebellion attempts to overthrow existing leadership by war, often prolonged. Revolution may involve these forms of violence, but includes the ingredient of ideology. The vital impulse in revolution is a reorientation of the value system based on a new world-view. The French and Bolshevik revolutions remain archetypes of this kind of political change, which commonly requires years for its completion. What coups d'état, rebellions, and revolutions share in common is their internality; they take place within a political community and seek a rearrangement of its power and authority.

A civil war of the American model is distinct from these kinds of violence in that those who commence it do not seek a rearrangement of power or ideology within the community, but rather a separate sovereignty over a particular geographical area. The parties seeking independence from a central authority usually share basic interests, background, beliefs and culture, and reject the established sovereign. The American Civil War was, in this special sense, a civil war, not a rebellion. (The American Revolution was also, strictly speaking, a civil war, not a revolution; no great value reorientation was intended or occurred in the territorial separation of sovereignty.)

Lincoln steadfastly maintained that the original compact of states was an intended and ratified union of people, not a contract among sovereign political units. He cited the *Preamble* to the Constitution, "We the People of the United States, in order to form a more perfect Union . . . " as proof that the founders' intent was an indissoluble union of citizens. The Articles of Confederation had joined the states in compact, but its successor, the Constitution, was intended to provide what its *Preamble* declared: a more perfect union of all citizens, regardless of geographical location or previous state allegiance. It followed logically that for one group of citizens to seek dismemberment of their established union was an act of treason against the whole community and consigned its perpetrators to the category of rebels, that is, criminals. The conclusion of this line of reasoning was that the conflict was an internal matter, to be settled by the policing force, that is, the Union Army, the agent of the authority of the whole union.

Constitutional scholars have contended that Lincoln's position was at least questionable; it rested on one of several interpretations of the intentions and motives of the founding fathers and was neither more nor less valid than the opposing interpretations of Southern spokesmen like John C. Calhoun, who argued for the abrogation of a contract among the states if, as in any legal contract, one or the other party failed to live up to its agreed obligations. The debate was resolved historically, mere arguments failing, and Lincoln preserved the Union partly by denying the Confederate states public status in international law. Had the Confederacy gained this status, which it avidly sought, and had France and Great Britain, the chief European powers, recognized the Confederacy as a sovereign country, the complete Union naval blockade of Confederate ports might have been challenged in international law, and a stoppage or seizure of neutral ships by the North could have been considered an act of war against the nations whose ships were so abused. But the neutral powers would not risk Union hostility (nor, perhaps, would Britain interpret international law in a way that might limit her own dominant sea power). The international stature and material resources which recognition would have provided were denied to the Confederacy. The Southern uprising was doomed.

Meanwhile, more local questions of prisoner exchange and parole arose. After the battle of Bull Run in 1861, the issue was whether or not prisoners could be exchanged between the warring parties without implicit recognition of Confederate sovereignty. Lieber solved the difficulty. After consulting international legal texts, he concluded that the customary rules of war and prisoner treatment should be observed for humanitarian reasons but would not constitute recognition of the rebels as true belligerents in international law, nor would the United States forfeit the right to try the rebels for treason. He published his opinions in an open letter to U.S. Attorney General Edward Bates in the New York newspapers in August 1861. It subsequently became official policy.[12]

A thornier problem ensued: the definition of guerrilla warfare and the status of the guerrilla. Union Army attitude and policy tended to equate all irregular troops with guerrillas, who in turn were classified as criminals. This vague generalization not only applied to those who actually bore arms in the Confederate cause, but also to noncombatant civilians who either actively or passively supported irregular troops. It was to this situation that Lieber's concise and lucid essay, *Guerrilla Parties Considered with Reference to the Laws and Usages of War*, was addressed. In the form of a lengthy letter, it was a response to Halleck's request accomplished in a remarkably few pages and with a precision of definition and historical example which modern treatises have hardly improved.

After reviewing the origin and meaning of the term "guerrilla" from its Spanish origin, he says:

> It is universally understood in this country at the present time that a guerrilla party means an irregular band of armed men, carry-

> ing on an irregular war, not being able, according to their character as a guerrilla party, to carry on what the law terms a regular war.

Lieber goes on to distinguish the following as "irregulars:"

> The freebooter, the marauder, the brigand, the partisan, the free corps, the spy, the rebel, the conspirator, the robber, and especially the highway robber, the rising en masse, or the "arming of the peasants."[13]

The originality of Lieber, not so much in military practice as in law, is accurately conveyed in his opening paragraph:

> The subject is substantially a new topic in the law of war, and it is, besides, exposed to the mischievous process . . . of throwing the mantel of a novel term around an old and well-known offense, in the expectation that a legalizing effect will result from the adoption of a new word having a technical sound . . . [14] The question how captured guerrilleros ought to be treated was not much discussed in the last century and . . . the whole discussion in the law of war is new. This will not surprise us when we consider that so justly celebrated a publicist as Bynkershoeck defended, as late as the beginning of last century, the killing of common prisoners of war.[15]

Later, in a letter on his "General Orders, no. 100" to Halleck on February 20, 1863, he added:

> . . . you, well-read in the literature of this branch of international law, know that nothing of the kind exists in any language. I had no guide, no groundwork, no text-book . . . Usage, history, reason, and conscientiousness, a sincere love of truth, justice and civilization have been my guides.[16]

Perhaps the most important distinction which Lieber attempted was that between "partisan" and "guerrilla:" "It has been stated that the word guerrilla is not only used for individuals engaged in petty war, but frequently as an equivalent of partisan." "General Halleck," he remarks, "seems to consider partisan troops and guerrilla troops as the same and seems to consider 'self-constitution' a characteristic of the partisan; while other legal and military writers define partisan as I have stated, namely, a soldier belonging to a corps which operates in the manner given . . .[17]

> Sometimes . . . partisan is used for a self-constituted guerrilla; more frequently it has a different meaning . . . The partisan leader commands a corps whose object is to injure the enemy by action separate from that of his own main army; the partisan acts chiefly upon the enemy's lines of connection and communication, and outside of or beyond the lines of connection of his own army, in the rear and on the flanks of the enemy. Rapid and varying movements and surprises are the chief means of his success; but he is part and parcel of the army, and, as such, considered entitled to the privileges of the law of war, so long as he does not transgress it.[18]

The clear implication in Lieber's discussion is that he views "partisans" as part of an official army and, though detached from it, *officially identifiable as such.* Though he does not mention him it is likely that Col. John Mosby, the Confederate known as the "Gray Ghost," who harassed Sheridan's troops, would have satisfied Lieber's criteria as a partisan; so too would the Yugoslavs commanded by Mihailovich and by Tito in World War II. "If the term partisan is used in the sense in which I have defined it, it is not necessary to treat of it specially."[19]

But the guerrilla is another matter:

> It is different if we understand by guerrilla parties, self-constituted sets of armed men in times of war, who form no integrant part of the organized army, do not stand on the regular pay-roll of the army, or are not paid at all, take up arms and lay them down at intervals, and carry on petty war (guerrilla) chiefly by raids, extortion, destruction, and massacre, and who cannot encumber themselves with many prisoners, and will therefore generally give no quarter.[20]

Again Lieber gives no specific examples, but certainly a group such as the notorious Quantrill's Raiders operating in the Kansas and Missouri territories would have met his definition of guerrilla (as well as his definitions for "free-booters" and "bushwackers").

Lieber was not presuming to lay down fixed dicta from theory to apply without question to any international situation, much less to the existing conflict, which he deemed internal. He was flexible and circumspect, if humane in intention, in the application of his concepts.

> I have thus endeavored to ascertain what may be considered the law of war or fair rules of action toward so-called guerrilla parties. I do not enter upon a consideration of their application to the civil war in which we are engaged. . . .[21]

In an internal war the treatment of the insurgents "is always undefined, and depends upon relaxations of the municipal law, suggested by humanity. . . ."

Yet we see again his ambivalence and a will to punish for crimes:

> How far rules which have formed themselves in the course of time between belligerents might be relaxed with safety toward the evildoers in our civil war; or how far such relaxation or mitigation would be likely to produce a beneficial effect upon an enemy who, in committing a great and bewildering wrong, seems to have withdrawn himself from the common influences of fairness, sympathy, truth, and logic—how far this ought to be done at the present moment must be decided by the executive power, civil and military, or possibly by the legislative power. It is not for me in [this] place to make the inquiry. So much is certain, that no army, no society engaged in war, any more than a society at peace, can allow unpunished assassination, robbery, and devastation without the deepest injury to itself and disastrous consequences which might change the very issue of the war.[22]

iv

Lieber's essay *Guerrilla Parties* was intended to place the making of policy in the definition and treatment of guerrillas in the hands of the civilian authority, providing guidelines, but with considerable latitude for intelligent interpretation according to circumstances. In so doing, it also brought him into close cooperation with official Washington, especially with Halleck. With this task completed he turned his attention to his "little book on the Laws and Usages of War" and an important correspondence with Halleck.

Shipping Instructions for HOGLEBKS

Print this Packing Slip and enclose inside the front cover of the book.

Please ship this item no later than Fri Sep 25, 2026.

Ship to:

ALIBRIS APEX DC 76926402-50
APEX
800 AVONDALE AVE.
GRANDVIEW HEIGHTS, OH 43212-3473
UNITED STATES

PN #	Item ID	Alibris ID	Media Type	Title / Author	Seller List Price	Order Date
76926402-50	Alibris.I2018x0000039	B084320836	BOOK	Lieber's Code and the Law of War Hartigan, Richard Shelley	$90.00	Sep, 15 2026

76926402-50

Between October 21, 1861, and February 6, 1862, when the war was only months old, Lieber had delivered a series of lectures at Columbia College on the "Law and Usages of War," with "Twenty-Seven Definitions and Elementary Positions Concerning the Laws and Usages of War."[23] Some of them appeared in the *New York Times*[24] and came to the attention of Halleck, whose own book, *International Law*,[25] had established him as a scholar in the field. Halleck wrote to Lieber for a brief of his lectures.[26] Before Lieber could respond he learned of his son's wounding at Fort Donelson and went west to be with him. During this trip, he and Halleck first met, the latter having been posted to command the western armies. Admirers of each other's works, they became friends. One result of this relationship was Lieber's essay on guerrilla warfare, requested by Halleck; the final result was to be Lieber's Code.

When Halleck was installed as General-in-Chief of the Union Armies, Lieber wrote to him, November 13, 1862:

> Ever since the beginning of our present War, it has appeared clearer and clearer to me, that the President ought to issue a set of rules and definitions providing for the most urgent cases, occurring under the Laws and Usages of War, and on which our Articles of War are silent. The last phases of our war, and the things which have come to light by the recent inquiries into the conduct of certain officers, have at length induced me to write to you on the subject. I address you as the jurist, no less than as the soldier.[27]

He proposed the formation of a committee of three with Halleck as chairman to draw up a code defining, under the laws of war, combatant offenses and appropriate punishments. He suggested such topics as who is a spy, and who shall be treated as prisoners of war. Lieber then returned to a preoccupying theme, the absence of any such code in other countries.

> I do not know that any such thing as I design, exists in any other country, but in all other countries the Law of War is much more reduced to naked Force or Might, than we are willing to do it, especially now, perhaps, in this Civil War, and there exists much

> more thorough organization in those countries, nor do single wars extend there over such distances as here.[28]

Halleck replied on November 15 in a friendly but terse manner: "I have no time at present to consider the subject mentioned in the paper enclosed,"[29] but Lieber was not to be put off. There followed an amusing contretemps between an obviously sincere but very hard-pressed general attempting to direct a war and an equally sincere, determined, and aging law professor who sensed that the time had come for the realization of a major personal goal if only his friend would act. Lieber wrote:

> I dare say that in the peculiar American division of public labour or, I should rather say, overwhelming concentration of labour, you cannot find time to reflect on a propostion such as I lately made to you. I shall not make it to the Secretary of War, or to the President; for I think it is you from whom the movement ought to have proceeded. I am sorry; for, the more I reflect on the matter, the more important it appears to me.[30]

After another exchange, in which Lieber asked Halleck to take his suggestion "out of the pigeon hole of your mind,"[31] Halleck appointed Lieber "to a special board created by the War Department 'to propose amendments or changes in the Rules and Articles of War and a code of regulations for the government of Armies in the field as authorized by the laws and usages of War.' "[32]

On the surface it appears that the primary goal, at this time, was to produce a set of regulations to make the Union Army a more efficient fighting machine, which would in turn make it more quickly victorious. A quirk of circumstances changed this limited goal and allowed Lieber the latitude to produce a more wide-ranging work. The Board was chaired by General Ethan Allen Hitchcock. Three other military men were included, Lieber being the only civilian.[33] Two were lawyers and one was a former instructor at West Point. All were able. Lieber initially circulated a memorandum suggesting changes in the internal military system, including a new curriculum for West Point. Instead of acting on his memorandum, the Board decided to attempt a revision and systematization of all the rules that had governed land warfare and appointed Lieber to prepare a draft. After several revisions and additions, some by Halleck, the final draft was approved by Lincoln on April 24, 1863 as "General Orders, no. 100: Instructions for the Government of Armies of the United States in the Field."[34] Thus was born Lieber's Code.

> Part propaganda and part expediency, but almost entirely sound international law at the core, the code was, like its chief author's personality, an admixture of military sternness with basic humanitarianism.[35]

The document was divided into ten sections with 157 articles. Frank Freidel states that "Perhaps one of the greatest merits of the order was its form. It was less a rigid legal code than a persuasively written essay on the ethics of conducting war."[36] This compliment gives the impression that the code was a somewhat idealistic, neochivalric statement, but in fact the code is a concise and careful rendering of international legal theory and practice up to Lieber's time. Freidel is correct in pointing out, however, that Lieber left the door open to interpretation and that two of the subjects which he treated, "military necessity" and "retaliation," were formulated in such a way that in some circumstances, commanders and soldiers could justify extreme severity toward the enemy.

Lieber wrote at the outset, "To save the country is paramount to all other considerations." He also defined military necessity as "those measures which are indispensable for securing the end of the war." In the next article he adds that "Military necessity admits of all direct destruction of life or limb of armed enemies, and of other persons whose destruction is incidentally unavoidable in the armed contests of the war"; but he concludes it with the admonition that "Men who take up arms against one another in public war do not cease on this account to be moral beings, responsible to one another and to God." Military necessity "does not admit of cruelty—that is the infliction of suffering for the sake of suffering or for revenge"; but it is "lawful to starve the hostile belligerent, armed or unarmed, so that it leads to the speedier subjection of the enemy." Military necessity does not allow "poison in any way, or wanton devastation of a district." "It admits of deception; but disclaims acts of perfidy; and in general . . . does not include any act of hostility which makes the return to peace unnecessarily difficult." Though precise in many other instances, there is no doubt that Lieber ambivalently provides great latitude as to what constitutes "cruelty," "perfidy," and "hostility."[37]

Retaliation against an enemy is another difficult category. It is never to be resorted to "as a measure of mere revenge, but only as a means of protective retribution, and moreover cautiously and unavoidably . . . retaliation shall only be resorted to after careful inquiry into the real occurrence and the character of the misdeeds that may demand retribution." "The laws of war can no more wholly dispense with retaliation than can the law of nations, of which it is a branch. Yet civilized nations acknowledge retaliation as the sternest feature of war." "Unjust or inconsiderate retaliation removes the belligerents farther and farther from the mitigating rules of regular war, and by rapid steps leads them nearer to the internecine wars of savages." Having implicitly looked back, Lieber characteristically expressed a reigning idea of progress:

> Modern times are distinguished from earlier ages by the existence at one and the same time of many nations and great governments related to one another in close intercourse. Peace is their normal condition; war is the exception. The ultimate object of all modern war is a renewed state of peace.

To this he added an observation that seems odd, written as it was near the midpoint of a long and bloody civil war: "The more vigorously wars are pursued the better it is for humanity. Sharp wars are brief."[38]

In section II Lieber discussed the protection of persons, religion, and the arts and sciences, and "punishment of crimes against the inhabitants of hostile countries." Works of art, libraries, telescopes and hospitals "must be secured against all avoidable injury, even when they are contained in fortified places whilst besieged or bombarded."[39] But perhaps the most compelling articles expressed Lieber's anti-slavery commitment:

> Slavery, complicating and confounding the ideas of property (that is, of a thing), and of personality (that is, of humanity), exists according to municipal or local law only. The law of nature and nations has never acknowledged it.[40]

Writing not only a general code but one for a specific war, he claimed:

> Therefore, in a war between the United States and a belligerent which admits of slavery, if a person held in bondage by that belligerent be captured by or come as a fugitive under the protection of the military forces of the United States, such person is immediately entitled to the rights and privileges of a free man.[41]

This statement is vintage Lieber, not necessarily international law theory. But it also coincided with Lincoln's thinking and policy in publishing the Emancipation Proclamation of January 1, 1863, three months before he signed "General Orders, no. 100." Salmon P. Chase, Secretary of the Treasury, and a Radical Republican, recorded Lincoln's thoughts on his forthcoming Proclamation, expressed to his Cabinet as early as September 22, 1862.

> When the rebel army was at Frederick, I determined, as soon as it should be driven out of Maryland, to issue a Proclamation of Emancipation such as I thought most likely to be useful. I said nothing to any one; but I made the promise to myself, and (hesitating a little)—to my Maker. The rebel army is now driven out, and I am going to fulfill that promise.[42]

In the next section, in which he deals with deserters, prisoners of war and hostages, Lieber added an attack on racism: "The law of nations knows no distinction of color, and if an enemy of the United States should enslave and sell any captured persons of their Army, it would be a case for the severest retaliation."[43]

Again, as often, Lieber commented optimistically that in modern war the killing of the enemy is not the object. "The destruction of the enemy in war . . . is a means to obtain that object of the belligerent which lies beyond the war, i.e., peace. Unnecessary or revengeful destruction of life is not lawful." The prisoner is to be well treated, clothed, fed and housed, and though he may be killed in the act of escape, "neither death nor any other punishment shall be inflicted upon him simply for his attempt to escape, which the law of war does not consider a crime."[44]

Sections IV, V and VI deal briefly with the definitions and status of partisans, "war-rebels," spies, flags of truce and exchange of prisoners. Perhaps Lieber felt that he could afford brevity, having covered so much of the same ground in his essay on guerrilla warfare. His short discussion of prisoner exchange would eventually lead to one of the greatest controversies between the armies of the North and South.[45] Exchange should take place "number for number—rank for rank—wounded for wounded."[46] He then turned his attention, and much space, to a subject which, by the standards of twentieth century war, seems almost amusingly archaic: the parole; later sections deal with armistice, capitulation, and assassination.

At the close, Lieber takes up insurrection, civil war and rebellion. The first he defines as "a rising of people in arms against their government, or a portion of it, or against one or more of its laws, or against an officer or officers of the government." Of the range of possible conflicts (as analyzed above), Lieber's definition would include coup d'état and rebellion. His definitions of civil war and rebellion require full quotation and careful analysis. A civil war for Lieber is:

> War between two or more portions of a country or state, each contending for the mastery of the whole, and each claiming to be the legitimate government. The term is also sometimes applied to war of rebellion, when the rebellious province or portions of the state are contiguous to those containing the seat of government. The term rebellion is applied to an insurrection of a large extent, and is usually a war between the legitimate government of a country and portions of provinces of the same who seek to throw off their allegiance to it and set up a government of their own.[47]

Lieber's commitment to a stable order and united community of free men blurred his definitions. He could not admit that the Confederacy was other than rebellious against the "legitimate government," hence his definitions of civil war and rebellion blur together. His description of rebellion is more appropriate to a true civil war: contiguous areas denying allegiance to an established government. This is what the Confederacy sought, not, as in the instance of Lieber's definition of civil war, "mastery of the whole and each claiming to be the [sole] legitimate government." To Lieber, nevertheless, the confederates were rebels, subject to the municipal law of the United States, and enjoyed no status as belligerents in international law. Still, even rebels deserved treatment in accord with the accepted customs and theory of land warfare; fundamental humanity required this. But such treatment in no way implied "a partial or complete acknowledgement of their government . . . as an independent or sovereign power." Moreover:

> Treating in the field the rebellious enemy according to the law and usages of war has never prevented the legitimate government from trying the leaders of the rebellion or chief rebels for high treason, and from treating them accordingly, unless they are included in a general amnesty.

To thwart a recognition of the Confederacy by France and Great Britain, Lieber added: "Neutrals have no right to make the adoption of the rules of war by the assailed government toward rebels, the ground of their own acknowledgement of the revolted people as an independent power."[48]

Perhaps the most important statements in the Lieber Code are his dicta on the civilian. These succinctly summarize a centuries-old effort by international legal theorists to distinguish and immunize those who did not actively participate in combat. In the opening section he states:

> The citizen or native of a hostile country is thus an enemy, as one of the constituents of the hostile state or nation; and as such is subjected to the hardships of the war. Nevertheless, as civilization has advanced during the last centuries, so has likewise steadily

> advanced, especially in war on land, the distinction between the private individual belonging to a hostile country and the hostile country itself, with its men in arms. The principle has been more and more acknowledged that the unarmed citizen is to be spared in person, property, and honor as much as the exigencies of war will admit.[49]

Appropriately, his final words also were addressed to the status of the noncombatant:

> All enemies in regular war are divided into two general classes—that is to say, into combatants and non-combatants or unarmed citizens of the hostile government. The military commander . . . distinguishes between the loyal citizen . . . and the disloyal citizen. The disloyal citizens may further be classified into those citizens known to sympathize with the rebellion without positively aiding it, and those who, without taking up arms, give positive aid and comfort to the rebellious enemy without being bodily forced thereto.[50]

For centuries writers had labored to develop the distinction between the proper targets of military violence, the armed or supporting fighting force, and the unarmed, non-resisting members of the enemy citizenry. The theorists had done their job well, but if actual military practices conformed with their ideas, it was largely accidental; now for the first time, with Lieber's Code, a nation's official policy was meant to coincide with their theories.

Although "General Orders, no. 100" enjoyed the status of an official order of the United States government, it did not receive immediate recognition from Union commanders. Confederate officials dismissed it as propagandistic and as allowing too much latitude to Union troops in occupied Southern territory. This was predictable, since Lieber so forcefully denied belligerent status to the Confederacy; the South could not accept his consignment of it to the position of rebellious provinces. Confederates also complained that, for example, the hated Union General, Ben Butler, operated within the letter of the Code's provisions while violating its spirit.[51] Lieber, himself, recognized that the generality of his rules, in the climate of war, provided for a range of interpretation in specific instances. To prevent abuses of the spirit of the code he continually appealed to the humanitarian instincts of intelligent and reasonable combatants. He was not naive enough to suppose that all commanders would opt for the humanitarian alternatives; but these were at least available and encouraged, and cruelty limited and discouraged. Balancing latitude with precision, the Code provided a guide that had never existed before, one for which Confederate officials should have been grateful; for, imperfect as it was, and not always adhered to, it was far better than the pre-existing formal vacuum. Lieber was fully aware of the Code's limitations and was not being falsely modest when he termed it "our little pamphlet . . . short but pregnant and weighty like some stumpy Dutch woman when in the family way with coming twins."[52]

The ill-assorted "twins" were military necessity and retaliation versus humanity and reconciliation. Sherman's march through Georgia did not technically violate the letter of the Code, with the exception of his unannounced and unnecessary bombardment of Atlanta. (Forty years later, in their next foreign war, "American army officers operating under General Orders 100 pleaded exoneration from charges of torturing Filipinos on the basis of this selfsame 'military necessity'.")[53]

While the Confederates derided it and the Union army applied it loosely, the Code was quickly adopted for a controversial purpose by the United States Supreme Court. In the first of two famous civil liberties cases arising from Lincoln's suspension of habeas corpus and the establishment of military trial commissions with jurisdiction over civilians and civil authorities, the court applied the Code. The case, *Ex parte Vallandigham*, pitted a former Democratic congressman from Ohio, who had outspokenly criticized the administration, against the government, over the issue of the constitutionality of the military trial commissions in areas under secure government control. Vallandigham, found guilty of disloyal sentiment by such a commission, was sentenced to confinement for the duration of the war. The Supreme Court refused to review the case but cited "General Orders, no. 100" in defense of the army's right to establish such commissions.[54] Lieber, the civil libertarian and nationalist, might well have agonized over this decision and the place of his work in it.

By the time peace returned, appreciation was growing for Lieber's Code. Supreme Court Chief Justice Salmon P. Chase called it a great work.[55] Lieber's own prediction to Halleck, "It will be adopted as a basis for similar works by the English, French, and Germans," soon proved correct.[56] The German theorist, Johann K. Bluntschli, long a correspondent of Lieber's, wrote a full-length work on international law in which the section on land warfare was little more than a translation of Lieber's Code. Finally, to complete what Lieber referred to as a "clover leaf" of international law, the distinguished French writer, Edward Laboulaye, translated Bluntschli's book into French.[57]

Lieber's work and ideas gained wider recognition in practice. The Prussian Army adopted the Code to govern its forces in the Franco-Prussian War of 1870. A congress of scholars used the Code at the Brussels Conference of 1874 as the basis for an attempted codification of the rules of land warfare. "The Russian delegate, Baron Jomini, as president of the conference, declared that the project of an international convention then present had its origin in the rules of President Lincoln."[58] Although the Brussels Conventions were not ratified, in 1880 the Institute of International Law made them, with Lieber's contributions, the basis for a manual of the laws of land warfare. Finally, with the landmark Hague Conventions of 1899 and 1907, Lieber's ideas found international expression. Lieber's originality and influence have been testified to by many writers. To cite but one example, Fredric de Martens wrote:

> So it is to the United States of North America and to President Lincoln that belongs the honor of having taken the initiative in defining with precision the customs and laws of war. This first official attempt to codify the customs of war and to collect in a code the rules binding upon military forces has notably contributed to impress the character of humanity upon the conduct of the northern states in the course of that war.[59]

"General Orders, no. 100" has endured as an ideal. The Code was the standard instruction for the United States Army during the Spanish-American War; when a new field manual was adopted in 1914, it incorporated everything practicable from the original Code. "As late as 1925 an instructor at the Army Service Schools, Fort Leavenworth, lauded it as 'probably the most important of all documents on the subject of the rules of land warfare.' " As late as World War II, the United States army *Field Manual* directly incorporated Lieber's work.[60]

If Lieber's text has now been stylistically superseded, his intent has not. *The Geneva Convention Relative to the Protection of Civilian Persons in Time of War* binds its signators as follows:

> 1) Persons taking no active part in the hostilities, including members of armed forces who have laid down their arms and those placed hors de combat by sickness, wounds, detention, or any other cause, shall in all circumstances be treated humanely, without any adverse distinction founded on race, colour, religion or faith, sex, birth or wealth, or any other similar criteria.
>
> To this end, the following acts are and shall remain prohibited at any time and in any place whatsoever with respect to the above-mentioned persons:
>
> a) violence to life and person, in particular murder of all kinds, mutilation, cruel treatment and torture;
> b) taking of hostages;
> c) outrages upon personal dignity, in particular humiliating and degrading treatment;
> d) the passing of sentences and the carrying out of executions without previous judgment pronounced by a regularly constituted court, affording all the judicial guarantees which are recognized as indispensable by civilized peoples. . . .[61]

The echo of Lieber is clear and distinct.

V

Western history reveals, slowly developing in custom and practice, and theological and philosophical thought, a notion, then a principle, that persons who did not directly make war ought not to be subjected to the threat or reality of death or rapine. Though this principle has been and continues to be violated, especially in our century, it remains the single most important statement of man's attempt to limit his collective reciprocal violence. The principle, clearly elaborated in twentieth century declarations of land warfare and international law, states that civilians ought to be protected from despoliation of their persons and property. Yet, ever more destructive weapons systems and political and social turmoil have made this rule seem almost archaic.

The overflowing bookshelves of analysis stress that nuclear conflict would invite general catastrophe. The carnage would be enormous, the political or human gain negligible or nil. Yet the arms race continues unabated, not only among the superpowers, but with increasing pace among lesser powers as well. In the face of this spectre, the distinction between civilian and soldier is menaced. The bitter irony is that in the name of the civilian's protection, weapons have been built and their use threatened; yet if these weapons are used, the civilian's protection thereby vanishes. The civilian, and civilian values, would perish by the means designed to protect him and them. If there are future generations to view ours, they can only conclude that our logic was ludicrously and tragically flawed.

Another form of conflict, less portentous in scale and suddenness than nuclear warfare but almost as threatening to local civilian life, is guerrilla war. It is not unique to our period, but its incidence has never been so widespread. In many places it has effectively replaced the traditional mode of "conventional" war where armies faced each other in recognizable units and formations. Instead, the very essence of guerrilla conflict, the strength of the guerrilla, requires unrecognizability. To strike with surprise while retaining anonymity are the touchstones of guerrilla success. Anonymity and surprise require a civilian "sea" in which the guerrilla "fish" can swim, and in the process may mortally affect that civilian "sea." Neither the guerrilla nor his antagonist accords the civilian the highest priority as a category of persons who should be protected and spared. In guerrilla combat the neutral civilian is merely a means to be used, or if necessary, abused, to attain victory.

The United States did not invent guerrilla warfare (nor death camps), but it did invent nuclear weapons, which it alone has used against civilians, and it remains one of the powers prepared to use them. This is a tragic irony in the history of the first nation to adopt specific rules to control and limit the conduct of its armies toward the civilian population of its enemies. This definition and limitation aimed at sparing civilians and limiting destruction of life and property in war. No nation, kingdom or empire had ever before placed such strictures on its warriors; no previous government had ever bound itself formally in voluntary policy to practice humane treatment toward its enemies; and few documents in western history were to have such an impact on the modern law of land warfare as Francis Lieber's Code.

The twentieth century has not been kind to the civilian, in spite of its adoption of protective treaties and conventions. The twin policies of military necessity and retaliation threaten to overwhelm us. Lieber (like Clausewitz) hoped to control military means for a political purpose. Their successors in the theory and practice of warfare have been unable to do so securely. We have come to accept an Orwellian transverbalization or Nietszchean transvaluation: "peace" is the period during which nations prepare for war; "defense systems" are prepared to annihilate projected enemies—and threaten the "defended"; and civilians cease to be distinct from soldiers. Peace is attenuated, while weapons and strategies of destruction without limits become normal. Lieber's Code summarized two millenia in the development of a norm of civilian immunity, only to be threatened with obsolescence in a few decades. The degree to which his ideas and ideals have been endangered does not reflect upon their worth but rather on the juxtaposition of values which his successors have chosen, or succumbed to.

Lieber's values are not invalid in our age; fairness and mercy are always human needs. The Hague and Geneva Conventions incorporated Lieber's Code and declared that the civilian shall be protected. Yet the reality of contemporary political and military policy consciously ignores this immunity and prepares war "scenarios" which would destroy it. George Orwell has proved indeed to be our modern Cassandra, for "double-think" has become our habitual mode of thinking. Until the world's nations and parties curb their ambitions and furies sufficiently to civilize their militarisms instead of militarizing whole populations, we are locked into the frightful prospect of mutual extinction.[62]

This essay began with a quotation from Elihu Root; another one is appropriate to conclude it:

> When we recall the frightful cruelties upon combatants, upon prisoners, upon citizens, the overturning of all human rights to life and liberty and property, the fiendish malignity of oppression by brutal force, which have characterized the history of war, we cannot fail to set a high estimate upon the service of a man who gave form and direction and effectiveness to the civilizing movement by which man at his best, through the concurrence of nations, imposes the restraint of rules of right conduct, upon man at his worst, in the extreme exercise of force.[63]

Would that it were so.

Notes

1. Introductory communication from E. D. Townsend, Assistant Adjutant-General of the Union Armies, April 24, 1863, in *The War of the Rebellion: A Compilation of the Official Records of the Union and Confederate Armies* (Washington: Government Printing Office, 1899), Series III, Vol. iii, 148. Hereafter, citations from this series will be abbreviated *WR* with series, volume, and pages.
2. H. W. Halleck, *International Law; or, Rules Regulating the Intercourse of States in Peace and War* (New York: D. von Nostrand, 1861).
3. Halleck to Lieber, Aug. 6, 1862, *WR*, ser. III, vol. ii, 301.
4. Lieber to Sumner, Aug. 19, 1861, Lieber to Allibone, Aug. 19, 1861, Lieber Papers, Huntington Library, San Marino, California, hereafter *HL.*

5. See Richard Shelly Hartigan, *The Forgotten Victim: A History of the Civilian* (Chicago: Precedent, 1982).
6. E. von Vattel, *The Law of Nations* (Washington: Carnegie Institution, 1916), 282–3.
7. Carl von Clausewitz, *On War*, ed. by Anatol Rappoport (Penguin ed., 1979), 101.
8. Lieber's birthdate is in doubt. Elihu Root cites it as March 18, 1800. Root, *Addresses on International Subjects* (Freeport, N.Y.: Books for Libraries, 1969), 95. In the excellent biography *Francis Lieber*, by Frank Freidel (Baton Rouge: Louisiana State University Press, 1977), 1, the author gives it as 1798. Lieber died in October 1872.
9. For details of Lieber's life and activities see Freidel and Root, above.
10. Freidel, *Lieber*, and Bernard Edward Brown, *American Conservatives: The Political Thought of Francis Lieber and John W. Burgess* (New York: Columbia University Press, 1951). Also see James Turner Johnson, *Just War Tradition and the Restraint of War* (Princeton: Princeton University Press, 1981), chap. IX, and James F. Childress, "Francis Lieber's Interpretation of the Laws of War: General Orders No. 100 in the Context of His Life and Thought," *American Journal of Jurisprudence*, 1976, 34–70.
11. Lieber to Halleck, March 4, 1863, quoted in Freidel, *Lieber*, 317.
12. *Ibid.*, 320–1 and n. 8.
13. *WR*, ser. III, vol. ii, 302–3.
14. *Ibid.*, 301.
15. *Ibid.*, 306.
16. Lieber to Halleck, Feb. 20, 1863, Lieber Papers, *HL*.
17. *WR*, ser. III, vol. ii, 307.
18. *Ibid.*, 304.
19. *Ibid.*, 307.
20. *Ibid.*, 308.
21. *Ibid.*, 309. Note Lieber's use of the term "civil war" when in fact he did not recognize the Confederates to be secessionists in the sense in which I have defined participants in a civil war. For Lieber, the South was in rebellion.
22. *Ibid.*
23. Both manuscripts are among the Lieber Papers, Johns Hopkins University Library, Baltimore.
24. See Freidel, *Lieber*, 324, n. 18.
25. Above, note 2.

26. Lieber to Halleck, Jan. 30, 1862, Halleck to Lieber, Feb. 3 and 11, 1862, *HL*.
27. Lieber to Halleck, Nov. 13, 1862, *HL*.
28. *Ibid*.
29. Halleck to Lieber, Nov. 15, 1862, *HL*.
30. Lieber to Halleck, Nov. 20, 1862, *HL*.
31. Lieber to Halleck, Nov. 25, 1862, *HL*.
32. See Freidel, *Lieber,* 332 and n. 35.
33. See Freidel, *Lieber,* 332–3, esp. n. 36–37. The other committee members were George L. Hortsuff, John H. Martindale and George Cadwalader.
34. The document was published in May: *WR*, ser. III, vol. iii, 148.
35. Freidel, *Lieber,* 335.
36. *Ibid*.
37. *WR*, ser. III, vol. iii, 149–50.
38. *Ibid*.
39. *Ibid*., 151–2.
40. *Ibid*., 153. Lieber had apparently forgotten Aristotle's justification of enslavement, among others. Great Britain had only abolished slavery in the Empire in 1832. The international law theorists were, with the exception of Vitoria, noticeably quiet on the subject. Lieber was, of course, correct that the classic literature of international legal theory did not explicitly sanction slavery but did consider the institution a matter of local or municipal law.
41. *Ibid*.
42. Quoted in *Lincoln and the Civil War*, ed. by Courtland Candy (New York: Braziller, 1960), 287.
43. *WR*, ser. III, vol. iii, 155. Lieber was responding here to formal Confederate orders to execute captured Negro officers. There were already well-authenticated reports, historically confirmed, that Negro prisoners had indeed been killed or sold into slavery by the Confederates. See James M. McPherson, *The Negro's Civil War* (New York: Vintage, 1965), 174.
44. *WR*, 156.
45. See, e.g., the correspondence below between the Confederate and Union agents for exchange of prisoners.
46. *WR*, 159.
47. *Ibid*., 163.
48. *Ibid*.
49. *Ibid*., 150.

50. *Ibid.*, 163–4.
51. See, e.g., the discussion and citations in Freidel, *Lieber*, 337 ff.
52. Quoted *ibid.*
53. *Ibid.*, 336. During the so-called Phillipine Insurrection atrocities were reported on both sides. There were some courts martial of American soldiers, with doubtful results. See *American Imperialism and the Phillipine Insurrection*, ed. by Henry F. Graff (Boston: Little, Brown), 1969.
54. See *Ex Parte Vallandigham*, 1 Wallace 243 (1863). This opinion was substantially reversed two years later in *Ex Parte Milligan*, 4 Wallace 2 (1866).
55. Chase to Lieber, Oct. 8, 1866, *HL.*
56. Lieber to Halleck, May 29, 1863, *HL.*
57. Freidel, *Lieber*, 340–2; Root, *Addresses*, 93.
58. *Ibid.*
59. See also the testimony of Nys and Bluntschli, *ibid.*, 94–5; F. de Martens, "Précis du Droit des Gens Moderne de l'Europe," 1879.
60. Freidel, *Lieber*, 340; U.S. War Department, *Field Manual 27–10, Rules of Land Warfare* (Washington, 1940).
61. *The Geneva Convention Relative to the Protection of Civilian Persons in Time of War*, U. S. Department of the Army, Pamphlet 27–1 (Washington, 1956), 136.
62. See my extended discussion of these topics in *Forgotten Victim*, passim.
63. Root, *Addresses*, 95.

I Guerrilla Parties Considered with Reference to the Laws and Usages of War

by Francis Lieber

The position of armed parties loosely attached to the main body of the army, or altogether unconnected with it, has rarely been taken up by writers on the law of war. The term guerrilla is often inaccurately used, and its application has been particularly confused at the present time. From these circumstances arises much of the difficulty which presents itself to the publicist and martial jurist in treating of guerrilla parties. The subject is substantially a new topic in the law of war, and it is, besides, exposed to the mischievous process, so often employed in our day, of throwing the mantle of a novel term around an old and well-known offense, in the expectation that a legalizing effect will result from the adoption of a new word having a technical sound; an illustration of which occurred in the introduction of the Latin and rarer term repudiation to designate the old practice of dishonestly declining the payment of debts—an offense with which the world has been acquainted ever since men united in the bonds of society. We find that self-constituted bands in the South, who destroy the cotton stored by their own neighbors, are styled in the journals of the North as well as in those of the South guerrillas; while in truth they are, according to the common law—not of war only, but that of every society—simply armed robbers, against whom every person is permitted, or is in duty bound, to use all the means of defense at his disposal; as, in a late instance, even General Toombs, of Georgia, declared to a certain committee of safety of his State that he would defend the planting and producing of his cotton; though, I must own, he did not call the self-constituted committee guerrillas, but, if memory serves me right, scoundrels.

The term guerrilla is the diminutive of the Spanish word guerra, war, and means petty war; that is, war carried on by detached parties, generally in the mountains. It means, further, the party of men united under one chief engaged in petty war, which, in the eastern portion of Europe and the whole Levant is called a capitanery, a band under one capitano. The term guerrilla, however, is not applied in Spain to a single man of the party; such a person is called a guerrillero, or more frequently a partida, which means partisan. Thus, Napier, in speaking of the guerrilla in his History of the Peninsular War, uses, with rare exception, the term partidas for the chiefs and men engaged in the petty war against the French. It is worthy of notice that the dictionary of the Spanish academy gives, as the first meaning of the word guerrilla, "A party of light troops for reconnaissance, and opening the first skirmishes." I translate from an edition of 1826, published, therefore, long after the Peninsular war, through which the term guerrilla has passed over into many other European languages. Self-constitution is not a necessary element of the meaning given by the Spaniards or by many writers of other nations to the word guerrilla, although it is true that the guerrilla parties in the Peninsular war were nearly all self-constituted, since the old government had been destroyed; and the forces which had been called into existence by the provisional government were no more acknowledged by the French as regular troops than the self-constituted bands under leading priests, lawyers, smugglers, or peasants; because the French did not acknowledge the provisional Junta or Cortes. Many of the guerrilleros were shot when made prisoners, as the guerrilla chiefs executed French prisoners in turn. It is the state of things these bands almost always lead to, according to their inherent character; yet, when the partidas of Mina and Empecinado had swelled to the imposing number of twenty thousand and more, which fact of itself implies a certain degree of discipline, Mina made a regular treaty with the French for the passage of certain French goods through the lines, and on these the partisan leader levied regular duties according to a tariff agreed upon between the belligerents arrayed against one another in fierce hostility.

What, then, do we in the present time understand by the word guerrilla? In order to ascertain the law or to settle it according to elements already existing, it will be necessary ultimately to give a distinct definition; but it may be stated here that whatever may be our final definition, it is universally understood in this country at the present time that a guerrilla party means an irregular band of armed men, carrying on an irregular war, not being able, according to their character as a guerrilla party, to carry on what the law terms a regular war. The irregularity of the guerrilla party consists in its origin, for it is either self-constituted or constituted by the call of a single individual, not according to the general law of levy, conscription, or volunteering; it consists in its disconnection with the army as to its pay, provision, and movements, and it is irregular as to the permanency of the band, which may be dismissed and called again together at any time. These are, I believe, constituent ideas of the term guerrilla as now used. Other ideas are associated with the term, differently by different persons. Thus many persons associate the idea of pillage with the guerrilla band, because, not being connected with the regular army, the men cannot provide for themselves, except by pillage, even in their own country—acts of violence with which the Spanish guerrilleros sorely afflicted their own countrymen in the Peninsular war. Others connect with it the idea of intentional destruction for the sake of destruction, because the guerrilla chief cannot aim at any strategic advantages or any regular fruits of victory. Others, again, associate with it the idea of the danger with which the spy surrounds us, because he that to-day passes you in the garb and mien of a peaceful citizen, may to-morrow, as a guerrillaman, fire your house or murder you from behind the hedge. Others connect with the guerrillero the idea of necessitated murder, because guerrilla bands cannot encumber themselves with prisoners of war; they have, therefore, frequently, perhaps generally, killed their prisoners, and of course have been killed in turn when made prisoners, thus introducing a system of barbarity which becomes intenser in its demoralization as it spreads and is prolonged. Others, again, connect the ideas of general and heinous criminality, of robbery and lust with the term, because the organization of the party being but slight and the leader utterly dependent upon the band, little discipline can be enforced, and where no discipline is enforced in war a state of things results which resembles far more the wars recorded in

Froissart, or Comines, or the thirty-years' war, and the religious war in France, than the regular wars of modern times. And such a state of things results speedily, too; for all growth, progress, and rearing, moral or material, are slow; all destruction, relapse, and degeneracy fearfully rapid. It requires the power of the Almighty and a whole century to grow an oak tree; but only a pair of arms, an ax, and an hour or two to cut it down.

History confirms these associations, but the law of war as well as the law of peace has treated many of these and kindred subjects—acts justifiable, offensive, or criminal—under acknowledged terms, namely: The freebooter, the marauder, the brigand, the partisan, the free corps, the spy, the rebel, the conspirator, the robber, and especially the highway robber, the rising en masse, or the "arming of peasants."

A few words on some of these subjects will aid us in coming to a clearer understanding of the main topic which occupies our attention.

Freebooter is a term which was in common use in the English language at no very remote period; it is of rare use now, because the freebooter makes his appearance but rarely in modern times, thanks to the more regular and efficient governments and to the more advanced state of the law of war. From the freebooter at sea arose the privateer, for the privateer is a commissioned freebooter, or the freebooter taken into the service of the government by the letter of marque. The sea-gueux, in the revolution of the Netherlands, were originally freebooters at sea, and they were always treated when captured simply as freebooters. Wherever the freebooter is taken, at sea or on land, death is inflicted upon him now as in former times, for freebooters are nothing less than armed robbers of the most dangerous and criminal type, banded together for the purposes of booty and of common protection.

The brigand is, in military language, the soldier who detaches himself from his troop and commits robbery, naturally accompanied in many cases with murder and other crimes of violence. His punishment, inflicted even by his own authorities, is death. The word brigand, derived as it is from briguer, to beg, meant originally beggar, but it soon came to be applied to armed strollers, a class of men which swarmed in all countries in the middle ages. The term has, however, received a wider meaning in modern military terminology. He that assails the enemy without or against the authority of his own government is called, even though his object should be wholly free from any intention of pillage, a brigand, subject to the infliction of death if captured. When Major von Schill, commanding a Prussian regiment of huzzars, marched in the year 1809 against the French without the order of his government, for the purpose of causing a rising of the people in the north of Germany, while Napoleon was occupied in the south with Austria, Schill was declared by Napoleon and his brother a brigand, and the King of Westphalia, Jerome Bonaparte, offered a reward of 10,000 francs for his head. Schill was killed in battle; but twelve young officers of his troop, taken prisoners, were carried by the French to the fortress Wesel, where a court-martial declared them prisoners of war. Napoleon quashed the finding, ordered a new court-martial, and they were all shot as brigands. Napoleon is not cited here as an authority in the law of war; he and many of his generals frequently substituted the harshest violence for martial usages. The case is mentioned as an illustration of the meaning attached to the word brigand in the law of war, and of the fact that death is the acknowledged punishment for the brigand.

The terms partisan and free corps are vaguely used. Sometimes, as we shall see further on, partisan is used for a self-constituted guerrillero; more frequently it has a different meaning. Both partisan corps and free corps designate bodies detached from the main army; but the former term refers to the action of the troop, the latter to the composition. The partisan leader commands a corps whose object is to injure the enemy by action separate from that of his own main army; the partisan acts chiefly upon the enemy's lines of connection and communication, and outside of or beyond the lines of operation of his own army, in the rear and on the flanks of the enemy. Rapid and varying movements and surprises are the chief means of his success; but he is part and parcel of the army, and, as such, considered entitled to the privileges of the law of war, so long as he does not transgress it. Free corps, on the other hand, are troops not belonging to the regular army, consisting of volunteers, generally raised by individuals authorized to do so by the government, used for petty war, and not incorporated with the *ordre de bataille.* They were known in the middle ages. The French *compagnies franches* were free corps; but this latter term came into use only in the eighteenth century. They were generally in bad repute, given to pillage and other excesses; but this is incidental. There were many free corps in Germany opposed to Napoleon when that country rose against the French, but the men composing them were entitled to the benefits of the law of war, and generally received them when taken prisoner. These free corps were composed in many cases of high-minded patriots. The difficulty regarding free corps and partisans arises from the fact that their discipline is often lax, and used to be so especially in the last century, so that frequently they cannot cumber themselves with prisoners; and that even for their own support they are often obliged to pillage or to extort money from the places they occupy. They are treated, therefore, according to their deserts, on the principle of retaliation; but there is nothing inherently lawless or brigand-like in their character.

The spy, the rebel, and conspirator deserve notice in this place simply with reference to persons acting as such, and belonging to the population of the country or district occupied by a hostile force. A person dwelling in a district under military occupation and giving information to the government of which he was subject, but which has been expelled by the victorious invader, is universally treated as a spy—a spy of a peculiarly dangerous character. The most patriotic motives would not shield such a person from the doom of the spy. There have been high-minded and self-sacrificing spies, but when captured, even if belonging to the armies themselves, they have never been treated otherwise than as common spies. Even mere secret correspondence of a person in an occupied district with the enemy, though the contents of the correspondence may have been innocent, has subjected the correspondent to serious consequences, and sometimes to the rigor of martial law, especially if the offense be committed after a proclamation to the contrary. Prince Hatzfeld was appointed by the King of Prussia, on his leaving the capital after the battle of Jena, to conduct public affairs in Berlin until the city should be occupied by the French, and to send a report to the king every morning until the occupation by the enemy should have taken place. Prince Hatzfeld sent such a report to his own government, giving the number of the French who had arrived at Potsdam on the 24th of October, at 5 o'clock a.m.—that is, seven hours before the French vanguard entered Berlin. The letter fell into the hands of Napoleon. It is well known that the emperor, at the supplication of the princess, allowed her husband to escape the penalty of a spy. Whatever may be thought of the question, whether the prince, by sending the letter at the hour mentioned became a spy or not, no one has ever doubted that, had he secretly corresponded with his government after the occupation of Berlin by the French, giving information of the occupants, the French would have been justified in treating him as a spy. The spy becomes, in this case, peculiarly dangerous, making hostile use of the protection which by the modern law of war the victor extends to the persons and property of the conquered. Similar remarks apply to the rebel, taking the word in the primitive meaning of rebellare—that is, to return to war after having been conquered; and to conspiracies—that is, secret agreements leading to such resumption of arms in bands of whatever number, or, which is still worse, plans to murder from secret places.

This war-rebel, as we might term him, this renewer of war within an occupied territory, has been universally treated with the utmost rigor of the military law. The war-rebel exposes the occupying army to the greatest danger, and essentially interferes with the mitigation of the severity of war, which it is one of the noblest objects of the modern law of war to obtain. Whether the war-rebel rises on his own account, or whether he has been secretly called upon by his former government to do so, would make no difference whatever. The royalists who recently rose in the mountains of Calabria against the national government of Italy, and in favor of Francis, who had been their king until within a recent period, were treated as brigands and shot, unless, indeed, pardoned on prudential grounds.

The rising en masse, or "the arming of peasants," as it used to be called, brings us nearer to the subject of the guerrilla parties. Down to the beginning of the first French revolution, toward the end of last century, the spirit which pervaded all governments of the European continent was, that the people were rather the passive substratum of the State than an essential portion of it. The governments were considered to be the State; wars were chiefly cabinet wars, not national wars—not the people's affairs.

Moser, in his Contributions to the Latest European Law of Nations in Times of War (a German work, in 3 vols., from 1779–1781), gives remarkable instances of the claims which the conqueror was believed to have on the property and on the subjects of the hostile country. They were believed to be of so extensive a character that the French, when in Germany, during the seven-years' war, literally drafted Germans for the French army, and used them as their own soldiers—although, it must be added, loud complaints were made, and the French felt themselves obliged to make some sort of explanation. The same work contains instances of complaints being made against arming the peasants, or of levies en masse, as contrary to the law of nations; but Moser also shows that the Austrians employed the Tyrolese (always familiar with the use of the rifle) in war without any complaint of the adversary.

Since that time most constitutions contain provisions that the people have a right to possess and use arms; everywhere national armies have been introduced, and the military law of many countries puts arms into the hands of all. Austria armed the people as militia in 1805; Russia in 1812; and Prussia introduced the most comprehensive measure of arming the people in 1813. The militia proper was called landwehr, and those who were too old for service in the landwehr were intended to form the landsturm—citizens armed as well as the circumstances might permit, and to be used for whatever military service within their own province they might be found fit. It is true that the French threatened to treat them as brigands—that is to say, not to treat them as prisoners of war if captured. The French, however, were expelled from Germany and no opportunity was given to test their threat.

I believe it can be said that the most recent publicists and writers on international law agree that the rising of the people to repel invasion entitles them to the full benefits of the law of war, and that the invader cannot well inquire into the origin of the armed masses opposing him—that is to say, he will be obliged to treat the captured citizens in arms as prisoners of war so long as they openly oppose him in respectable numbers and have risen in the yet uninvaded or unconquered portions of the hostile country.

Their acting in separate bodies does not necessarily give them a different character. Some entire wars have been carried on by separate bands or capitaneries, such as the recent war of independence of Greece. It is true, indeed, that the question of the treatment of prisoners was not discussed in that war, because the Turkish Government killed or enslaved all prisoners; but I take it that a civilized government would not have allowed the fact that the Greeks fought in detached parties and carried on mountain guerrilla [war] to influence its conduct toward prisoners.

I may here observe that the question how captured guerrilleros ought to be treated was not much discussed in the last century and, comparatively, the whole discussion in the law of war is new. This will not surprise us when we consider that so justly celebrated a publicist as Bynkershoeck defended, as late as the beginning of last century, the killing of common prisoners of war.

It does not seem that, in the case of a rising en masse, the absence of a uniform can constitute a difference. There are cases, indeed, in which the absence of a uniform may be taken as very serious prima facie evidence against an armed prowler or marauder, but it must be remembered that a uniform dress is a matter of impossibility in a levy en masse; and in some cases regulars have had no uniforms, at least for a considerable time. The Southern prisoners made at Fort Donelson, whom I have seen at the West, had no uniforms. They were indeed dressed very much alike, but it was the uniform dress of the countryman in that region. Yet they were treated by us as prisoners of war, and well treated, too. Nor would it be difficult to adopt something of a badge, easily put on and off, and to call it a uniform. It makes a great difference, however, whether the absence of the uniform is used for the purpose of concealment or disguise, in order to get by stealth within the lines of the invader, for destruction of life or property, or for pillage, and whether the parties have no organization at all, and are so small that they cannot act otherwise than by stealth. Nor can it be maintained in good faith, or with any respect for sound sense and judgment, that an individual—an armed prowler—(now frequently called a bushwhacker) shall be entitled to the protection of the law of war simply because he says that he has taken up his gun in defense of his country, or because his government or his chief has issued a proclamation by which he calls upon the people to infest the bushes and commit homicides which every civilized nation will consider murders. Indeed, the importance of writing on this subject is much diminished by the fact that the soldier generally decides these cases for himself. The most disciplined soldiers will execute on the spot an armed and murderous prowler found where he could have no business as a peaceful citizen. Even an enemy in the uniform of the hostile army would stand little chance of protection if found prowling near the opposing army, separate from his own troops at a greater than picket distance, and under generally suspicious circumstances. The chance would, of course, be far less if the prowler is in the common dress worn by the countryman of the district. It may be added here that a person proved to be a regular soldier of the enemy's army found in citizens' dress within the lines of the captor is universally dealt with as a spy.

It has been stated that the word guerrilla is not only used for individuals engaged in petty war, but frequently as an equivalent of partisan. General Halleck, in his International Law, or Rules Regulating the Intercourse of States in Peace and War, San Francisco, 1861, page 386 *et seq.*, seems to consider partisan troops and guerrilla troops as the same, and seems to consider "self-constitution" a characteristic of the partisan; while other legal and military writers define partisan as I have stated, namely, a soldier belonging to a corps which operates in the manner given above. I beg the reader to peruse that passage, both on account of its own value and of the many important and instructive authorities which he will find there. They are collected with that careful industry which distinguishes the whole work.

Dr. T. D. Woolsey, page 299 *et seq.*, of his Introduction to the Study of International Law, Boston, 1860, says:

> The treatment which the milder modern usage prescribes for regular soldiers is extended also to militia called out by public authority. Guerrilla parties, however, do not enjoy the full benefit of the laws of war. They are apt to fare worse than either regular troops or an armed peasantry. The reasons for this are, that they are annoying and insidious; that they put on and off with ease the character of a soldier, and that they are prone themselves to treat their enemies who fall into their hands with great severity.

If the term partisan is used in the sense in which I have defined it, it is not necessary to treat of it specially. The partisan in this sense is, of course, answerable for the commission of those acts to which the law of war grants no protection, and by which the soldier forfeits being treated as a prisoner of war if captured.

It is different if we understand by guerrilla parties, self-constituted sets of armed men in times of war, who form no integrant part of the organized army, do not stand on the regular pay-roll of the army, or are not paid at all, take up arms and lay them down at intervals, and carry on petty war (guerrilla) chiefly by raids, extortion, destruction, and massacre, and who cannot encumber themselves with many prisoners, and will therefore generally give no quarter.

They are peculiarly dangerous because they easily evade pursuit, and by laying down their arms become insidious enemies; because they cannot otherwise subsist than by rapine, and almost always degenerate into simple robbers or brigands. The Spanish guerrilla bands against Napoleon proved a scourge to their own countrymen, and became efficient for their own cause only in the same degree in which they gradually became disciplined. The Royalists in the north of France during the first Revolution, although setting out with sentiments of loyal devotion to their unfortunate king, soon degenerated into bands of robbers, while many robbers either joined them or assumed the name of Royalists. Napoleon states that their brigandage gave much trouble and obliged the Government to resort to the severest measures.

For an account of the misdeeds and want of efficiency of the Spanish guerrilleros, the reader is referred to Napier's Peninsular War, and especially to Chapter II, Book XVII, [where] he will find, in Guizot's Memoirs, Volume IV, page 100 *et seq.*, that in the struggle between the Christinos and Carlists the guerrilla parties under Mina and Zumalacarreguy regularly massacred their mutual prisoners, until the evil became so revolting to the Spaniards themselves that a regular treaty was concluded between the parties, stipulating the exchange of prisoners immediately after being made. How the surplus on the one or the other side was dealt with I do not know, but the treaty, concluded after the butchering of prisoners had been going on for a long time, is mentioned in all the histories of that period.

But when guerrilla parties aid the main army of a belligerent it will be difficult for the captor of guerrillamen to decide at once whether they are regular partisans, distinctly authorized by their own government; and it would seem that we are borne out by the conduct of the most humane belligerents in recent times, and by many of the modern writers, if the rule be laid down, that guerrillamen, when captured in fair fight and open warfare, should be treated as the regular partisan is, until special crimes, such as murder, or the killing of prisoners, or the sacking of places, are proved upon them, leaving the question of self-constitution unexamined.

The law of war, however, would not extend a similar favor to small bodies of armed country people, near the lines, whose very smallness shows that they must resort to occasional fighting and the occasional assuming of peaceful habits, and to brigandage. The law of war would still less favor them when they trespass within the hostile lines to commit devastation, rapine, or destruction. Every European army has treated such persons, and it seems to me would continue, even in the improved state of the present usages of war, to treat them as brigands, whatever prudential mercy might decide upon in single cases. This latter consideration cannot be discussed here; it does not appertain to the law of war.

It has been stated already that the armed prowler, the so-called bushwhacker, is a simple assassin, and will thus always be considered by soldier and citizen; and we have likewise seen that the armed bands that rise in a district fairly occupied by military force, or in the rear of an army, are universally considered, if captured, brigands, and not prisoners of war. They unite the fourfold character of the spy, the brigand, the assassin, and the rebel, and cannot—indeed, it must be supposed, will not—expect to be treated as a fair enemy of the regular war. They know what a hazardous career they enter upon when they take up arms, and that were the case reversed they would surely not grant the privileges of regular warfare to persons who should thus rise in their rear.

I have thus endeavored to ascertain what may be considered the law of war or fair rules of action toward so-called guerrilla parties. I do not enter upon a consideration of their application to the civil war in which we are engaged, nor of the remarkable claims recently set up by our enemies, demanding us to act according to certain rules which they have signally and officially disregarded toward us. I have simply proposed to myself to find a certain portion of the law of war. The application of the laws and usages of war to wars of insurrection or rebellion is always undefined, and depends upon relaxations of the municipal law, suggested by humanity or necessitated by the numbers engaged in the insurrection. The law of war, as acknowledged between independent belligerents, is at times not allowed to interfere with the municipal law of rebellion, or is allowed to do so only very partially, as was the case in Great Britain during the Stuart rebellion, in the middle of last century; at other times, again, measures are adopted in rebellions, by the victorious party or the legitimate government, more lenient even than the international law of war. Neither of these topics can occupy us here, nor does the letter prefixed to this tract contain the request that I should do so. How far rules which have formed themselves in the course of time between belligerents might be relaxed with safety toward the evil-doers in our civil war, or how far such relaxation or mitigation would be likely to produce a beneficial effect upon an enemy who in committing a great and bewildering wrong seems to have withdrawn himself from the common influences of fairness, sympathy, truth, and logic—how far this ought to be done at the present moment must be decided by the executive power, civil and military, or possibly by the legislative power. It is not for me in this place to make the inquiry. So much is certain, that no army, no society engaged in war, any more than a society at peace, can allow unpunished assassination, robbery, and devastation without the deepest injury to itself and disastrous conseqences which might change the very issue of the war.

II General Orders No. 100

GENERAL ORDERS, No. 100.

WAR DEPT., ADJT. GENERAL'S OFFICE, *Washington, April 24, 1863.*

The following "Instructions for the Government of Armies of the United States in the Field," prepared by Francis Lieber, LL.D., and revised by a board of officers, of which Maj. Gen. E. A. Hitchcock is president, having been approved by the President of the United States, he commands that they be published for the information of all concerned.

By order of the Secretary of War:

E. D. TOWNSEND,
Assistant Adjutant-General.

INSTRUCTIONS FOR THE GOVERNMENT OF ARMIES OF THE UNITED STATES IN THE FIELD.

SECTION I.—*Martial law—Military jurisdiction—Military necessity—Retaliation.*

1. A place, district, or country occupied by an enemy stands, in consequence of the occupation, under the martial law of the invading or occupying army, whether any proclamation declaring martial law, or any public warning to the inhabitants, has been issued or not. Martial law is the immediate and direct effect and consequence of occupation or conquest.

The presence of a hostile army proclaims its martial law.

2. Martial law does not cease during the hostile occupation, except by special proclamation, ordered by the commander-in-chief, or by special mention in the treaty of peace concluding the war, when the occupation of a place or territory continues beyond the conclusion of peace as one of the conditions of the same.

3. Martial law in a hostile country consists in the suspension by the occupying military authority of the criminal and civil law, and of the domestic administration and government in the occupied place or territory, and in the substitution of military rule and force for the same, as well as in the dictation of general laws, as far as military necessity requires this suspension, substitution, or dictation.

The commander of the forces may proclaim that the administration of all civil and penal law shall continue either wholly or in part, as in times of peace, unless otherwise ordered by the military authority.

4. Martial law is simply military authority exercised in accordance with the laws and usages of war. Military oppression is not martial law; it is the abuse of the power which that law confers. As martial law is executed by military force, it is incumbent upon those who administer it to be strictly guided by the principles of justice, honor, and humanity—virtues adorning a soldier even more than other men, for the very reason that he possess the power of his arms against the unarmed.

5. Martial law should be less stringent in places and countries fully occupied and fairly conquered. Much greater severity may be exercised in places or regions where actual hostilities exist or are expected and must be prepared for. Its most complete sway is allowed—even in the commander's own country—when face to face with the enemy, because of the absolute necessities of the case, and of the paramount duty to defend the country against invasion.

To save the country is paramount to all other considerations.

6. All civil and penal law shall continue to take its usual course in the enemy's places and territories under martial law, unless interrupted or stopped by order of the occupying military power; but all the functions of the hostile government—legislative, executive, or administrative—whether of a general, provincial, or local character, cease under martial law, or continue only with the sanction, or, if deemed necessary, the participation of the occupier or invader.

7. Martial law extends to property, and to persons, whether they are subjects of the enemy or aliens to that government.

8. Consuls, among American and European nations, are not diplomatic agents. Nevertheless, their offices and persons will be subjected to martial law in cases of urgent necessity only; their property and business are not exempted. Any delinquency they commit against the established military rule may be punished as in the case of any other inhabitant, and such punishment furnishes no reasonable ground for international complaint.

9. The functions of ambassadors, ministers, or other diplomatic agents, accredited by neutral powers to the hostile government, cease, so far as regards the displaced government; but the conquering or occupying power usually recognizes them as temporarily accredited to itself.

10. Martial law affects chiefly the police and collection of public revenue and taxes, whether imposed by the expelled government or by the invader, and refers mainly to the support and efficiency of the Army, its safety, and the safety of its operations.

11. The law of war does not only disclaim all cruelty and bad faith concerning engagements concluded with the enemy during the war, but also the breaking of stipulations solemnly contracted by the belligerents in time of peace, and avowedly intended to remain in force in case of war between the contracting powers.

It disclaims all extortions and other transactions for individual gain; all acts of private revenge, or connivance at such acts.

Offenses to the contrary shall be severely punished, and especially so if committed by officers.

12. Whenever feasible, martial law is carried out in cases of individual offenders by military courts; but sentences of death shall be executed only with the approval of the chief executive, provided the urgency of the case does not require a speedier execution, and then only with the approval of the chief commander.

13. Military jurisdiction is of two kinds: First, that which is conferred and defined by statute; second, that which is derived from the common law of war. Military offenses under the statute

law must be tried in the manner therein directed; but military offenses which do not come within the statute must be tried and punished under the common law of war. The character of the courts which exercise these jurisdictions depends upon the local laws of each particular country.

In the armies of the United States the first is exercised by courts-martial; while cases which do not come within the Rules and Articles of War, or the jurisdiction conferred by statute on courts-martial, are tried by military commissions.

14. Military necessity, as understood by modern civilized nations, consists in the necessity of those measures which are indispensable for securing the ends of the war, and which are lawful according to the modern law and usages of war.

15. Military necessity admits of all direct destruction of life or limb of armed enemies, and of other persons whose destruction is incidentally unavoidable in the armed contests of the war; it allows of the capturing of every armed enemy, and every enemy of importance to the hostile government, or of peculiar danger to the captor; it allows of all destruction of property, and obstruction of the ways and channels of traffic, travel, or communication, and of all withholding of sustenance or means of life from the enemy; of the appropriation of whatever an enemy's country affords necessary for the subsistence and safety of the Army, and of such deception as does not involve the breaking of good faith either positively pledged, regarding agreements entered into during the war, or supposed by the modern law of war to exist. Men who take up arms against one another in public war do not cease on this account to be moral beings, responsible to one another and to God.

16. Military necessity does not admit of cruelty—that is, the infliction of suffering for the sake of suffering or for revenge, nor of maiming or wounding except in fight, nor of torture to extort confessions. It does not admit of the use of poison in any way, nor of the wanton devastation of a district. It admits of deception, but disclaims acts of perfidy; and, in general, military necessity does not include any act of hostility which makes the return to peace unnecessarily difficult.

17. War is not carried on by arms alone. It is lawful to starve the hostile belligerent, armed and unarmed, so that it leads to the speedier subjection of the enemy.

18. When a commander of a besieged place expels the non-combatants, in order to lessen the number of those who consume his stock of provisions, it is lawful, though an extreme measure, to drive them back, so as to hasten on the surrender.

19. Commanders, whenever admissible, inform the enemy of their intention to bombard a place, so that the non-combatants, and especially the women and children, may be removed before the bombardment commences. But it is no infraction of the common law of war to omit thus to inform the enemy. Surprise may be a necessity.

20. Public war is a state of armed hostility between sovereign nations or governments. It is a law and requisite of civilized existence that men live in political, continuous societies, forming organized units, called states or nations, whose constituents bear, enjoy, and suffer, advance and retrograde together, in peace and in war.

21. The citizen or native of a hostile country is thus an enemy, as one of the constituents of the hostile state or nation, and as such is subjected to the hardships of the war.

22. Nevertheless, as civilization has advanced during the last centuries, so has likewise steadily advanced, especially in war on land, the distinction between the private individual belonging to a hostile country and the hostile country itself, with its men in arms. The principle has been more and more acknowledged that the unarmed citizen is to be spared in person, property, and honor as much as the exigencies of war will admit.

23. Private citizens are no longer murdered, enslaved, or carried off to distant parts, and the inoffensive individual is as little disturbed in his private relations as the commander of the hostile troops can afford to grant in the overruling demands of a vigorous war.

24. The almost universal rule in remote times was, and continues to be with barbarous armies, that the private individual of the hostile country is destined to suffer every privation of liberty

and protection and every disruption of family ties. Protection was, and still is with uncivilized people, the exception.

25. In modern regular wars of the Europeans and their descendants in other portions of the globe, protection of the inoffensive citizen of the hostile country is the rule; privation and disturbance of private relations are the exceptions.

26. Commanding generals may cause the magistrates and civil officers of the hostile country to take the oath of temporary allegiance or an oath of fidelity to their own victorious government or rulers, and they may expel every one who declines to do so. But whether they do so or not, the people and their civil officers owe strict obedience to them as long as they hold sway over the district or country, at the peril of their lives.

27. The law of war can no more wholly dispense with retaliation than can the law of nations, of which it is a branch. Yet civilized nations acknowledge retaliation as the sternest feature of war. A reckless enemy often leaves to his opponent no other means of securing himself against the repetition of barbarous outrage.

28. Retaliation will therefore never be resorted to as a measure of mere revenge, but only as a means of protective retribution, and moreover cautiously and unavoidably—that is to say, retaliation shall only be resorted to after careful inquiry into the real occurrence and the character of the misdeeds that may demand retribution.

Unjust or inconsiderate retaliation removes the belligerents farther and farther from the mitigating rules of regular war, and by rapid steps leads them nearer to the internecine wars of savages.

29. Modern times are distinguished from earlier ages by the existence at one and the same time of many nations and great governments related to one another in close intercourse.

Peace is their normal condition; war is the exception. The ultimate object of all modern war is a renewed state of peace.

The more vigorously wars are pursued the better it is for humanity. Sharp wars are brief.

30. Ever since the formation and coexistence of modern nations, and ever since wars have become great national wars, war

has come to be acknowledged not to be its own end, but the means to obtain great ends of state, or to consist in defense against wrong; and no conventional restriction of the modes adopted to injure the enemy is any longer admitted; but the law of war imposes many limitations and restrictions on principles of justice, faith, and honor.

SECTION II.—*Public and private property of the enemy—Protection of persons, and especially of women; of religion, the arts and sciences—Punishment of crimes against the inhabitants of hostile countries.*

31. A victorious army appropriates all public money, seizes all public movable property until further direction by its government, and sequesters for its own benefit or of that of its government all the revenues of real property belonging to the hostile government or nation. The title to such real property remains in abeyance during military occupation, and until the conquest is made complete.

32. A victorious army, by the martial power inherent in the same, may suspend, change or abolish, as far as the martial power extends, the relations which arise from the services due, according to the existing laws of the invaded country, from one citizen, subject, or native of the same to another.

The commander of the army must leave it to the ultimate treaty of peace to settle the permanency of this change.

33. It is no longer considered lawful—on the contrary, it is held to be a serious breach of the law of war—to force the subjects of the enemy into the service of the victorious government, except the latter should proclaim, after a fair and complete conquest of the hostile country or district, that it is resolved to keep the country, district, or place permanently as its own and make it a portion of its own country.

34. As a general rule, the property belonging to churches, to hospitals, or other establishments of an exclusively charitable character, to establishments of education, or foundations for the promotion of knowledge, whether public schools, universities,

academies of learning or observatories, museums of the fine arts, or of a scientific character—such property is not to be considered public property in the sense of paragraph 31; but it may be taxed or used when the public service may require it.

35. Classical works of art, libraries, scientific collections, or precious instruments, such as astronomical telescopes, as well as hospitals, must be secured against all avoidable injury, even when they are contained in fortified places whilst besieged or bombarded.

36. If such works of art, libraries, collections, or instruments belonging to a hostile nation or government, can be removed without injury, the ruler of the conquering state or nation may order them to be seized and removed for the benefit of the said nation. The ultimate ownership is to be settled by the ensuing treaty of peace.

In no case shall they be sold or given away, if captured by the armies of the United States, nor shall they ever be privately appropriated, or wantonly destroyed or injured.

37. The United States acknowledge and protect, in hostile countries occupied by them, religion and morality; strictly private property; the persons of the inhabitants, especially those of women; and the sacredness of domestic relations. Offenses to the contrary shall be rigorously punished.

This rule does not interfere with the right of the victorious invader to tax the people or their property, to levy forced loans, to billet soldiers, or to appropriate property, especially houses, lands, boats or ships, and the churches, for temporary and military uses.

38. Private property, unless forfeited by crimes or by offenses of the owner, can be seized only by way of military necessity, for the support or other benefit of the Army or of the United States.

If the owner has not fled, the commanding officer will cause receipts to be given, which may serve the spoliated owner to obtain indemnity.

39. The salaries of civil officers of the hostile government who remain in the invaded territory, and continue the work of

their office, and can continue it according to the circumstances arising out of the war—such as judges, administrative or political officers, officers of city or communal governments—are paid from the public revenue of the invaded territory until the military government has reason wholly or partially to discontinue it. Salaries or incomes connected with purely honorary titles are always stopped.

40. There exists no law or body of authoritative rules of action between hostile armies, except that branch of the law of nature and nations which is called the law and usages of war on land.

41. All municipal law of the ground on which the armies stand, or of the countries to which they belong, is silent and of no effect between armies in the field.

42. Slavery, complicating and confounding the ideas of property (that is, of a thing), and of personality (that is, of humanity), exists according to municipal or local law only. The law of nature and nations has never acknowledged it. The digest of the Roman law enacts the early dictum of the pagan jurist, that "so far as the law of nature is concerned, all men are equal." Fugitives escaping from a country in which they were slaves, villains, or serfs, into another country, have, for centuries past, been held free and acknowledged free by judicial decisions of European countries, even though the municipal law of the country in which the slave had taken refuge acknowledged slavery within its own dominions.

43. Therefore, in a war between the United States and a belligerent which admits of slavery, if a person held in bondage by that belligerent be captured by or come as a fugitive under the protection of the military forces of the United States, such person is immediately entitled to the rights and privileges of a freeman. To return such person into slavery would amount to enslaving a free person, and neither the United States nor any officer under their authority can enslave any human being. Moreover, a person so made free by the law of war is under the shield of the law of nations, and the former owner or State can have, by the law of postliminy, no belligerent lien or claim of service.

44. All wanton violence committed against persons in the invaded country, all destruction of property not commanded by the authorized officer, all robbery, all pillage or sacking, even after taking a place by main force, all rape, wounding, maiming, or killing of such inhabitants, are prohibited under the penalty of death, or such other severe punishment as may seem adequate for the gravity of the offense.

A soldier, officer, or private, in the act of committing such violence, and disobeying a superior ordering him to abstain from it, may be lawfully killed on the spot by such superior.

45. All captures and booty belong, according to the modern law of war, primarily to the government of the captor.

Prize money, whether on sea or land, can now only be claimed under local law.

46. Neither officers nor soldiers are allowed to make use of their position or power in the hostile country for private gain, not even for commercial transactions otherwise legitimate. Offenses to the contrary committed by commissioned officers will be punished with cashiering or such other punishment as the nature of the offense may require; if by soldiers, they shall be punished according to the nature of the offense.

47. Crimes punishable by all penal codes, such as arson, murder, maiming, assaults, highway robbery, theft, burglary, fraud, forgery, and rape, if committed by an American soldier in a hostile country against its inhabitants, are not only punishable as at home, but in all cases in which death is not inflicted the severer punishment shall be preferred.

SECTION III.—*Deserters—Prisoners of war—Hostages—Booty on the battle-field.*

48. Deserters from the American Army, having entered the service of the enemy, suffer death if they fall again into the hands of the United States, whether by capture or being delivered up to the American Army; and if a deserter from the enemy, having taken service in the Army of the United States, is captured by

the enemy, and punished by them with death or otherwise, it is not a breach against the law and usages of war, requiring redress or retaliation.

49. A prisoner of war is a public enemy armed or attached to the hostile army for active aid, who has fallen into the hands of the captor, either fighting or wounded, on the field or in the hospital, by individual surrender or by capitulation.

All soldiers, of whatever species of arms; all men who belong to the rising en masse of the hostile country; all those who are attached to the Army for its efficiency and promote directly the object of the war, except such as are hereinafter provided for; all disabled men or officers on the field or elsewhere, if captured; all enemies who have thrown away their arms and ask for quarter, are prisoners of war, and as such exposed to the inconveniences as well as entitled to the privileges of a prisoner of war.

50. Moreover, citizens who accompany an army for whatever purpose, such as sutlers, editors, or reporters of journals, or contractors, if captured, may be made prisoners of war and be detained as such.

The monarch and members of the hostile reigning family, male or female, the chief, and chief officers of the hostile government, its diplomatic agents, and all persons who are of particular and singular use and benefit to the hostile army or its government, are, if captured on belligerent ground, and if unprovided with a safe-conduct granted by the captor's government, prisoners of war.

51. If the people of that portion of an invaded country which is not yet occupied by the enemy, or of the whole country, at the approach of a hostile army, rise, under a duly authorized levy, en masse to resist the invader, they are now treated as public enemies, and, if captured, are prisoners of war.

52. No belligerent has the right to declare that he will treat every captured man in arms of a levy en masse as a brigand or bandit.

If, however, the people of a country, or any portion of the same, already occupied by an army, rise against it, they are violators of the laws of war and are not entitled to their protection.

53. The enemy's chaplains, officers of the medical staff, apothecaries, hospital nurses, and servants, if they fall into the hands of the American Army, are not prisoners of war, unless the commander has reasons to retain them. In this latter case, or if, at their own desire, they are allowed to remain with their captured companions, they are treated as prisoners of war, and may be exchanged if the commander sees fit.

54. A hostage is a person accepted as a pledge for the fulfillment of an agreement concluded between belligerents during the war, or in consequence of a war. Hostages are rare in the present age.

55. If a hostage is accepted, he is treated like a prisoner of war, according to rank and condition, as circumstances may admit.

56. A prisoner of war is subject to no punishment for being a public enemy, nor is any revenge wreaked upon him by the intentional infliction of any suffering, or disgrace, by cruel imprisonment, want of food, by mutilation, death, or any other barbarity.

57. So soon as a man is armed by a sovereign government and takes the soldier's oath of fidelity he is a belligerent; his killing, wounding, or other warlike acts are no individual crimes or offenses. No belligerent has a right to declare that enemies of a certain class, color, or condition, when properly organized as soldiers, will not be treated by him as public enemies.

58. The law of nations knows of no distinction of color, and if an enemy of the United States should enslave and sell any captured persons of their Army, it would be a case for the severest retaliation, if not redressed upon complaint.

The United States cannot retaliate by enslavement; therefore death must be the retaliation for this crime against the law of nations.

59. A prisoner of war remains answerable for his crimes committed against the captor's army or people, committed before he was captured, and for which he has not been punished by his own authorities.

All prisoners of war are liable to the infliction of retaliatory measures.

60. It is against the usage of modern war to resolve, in hatred and revenge, to give no quarter. No body of troops has the right to declare that it will not give, and therefore will not expect, quarter; but a commander is permitted to direct his troops to give no quarter, in great straits, when his own salvation makes it impossible to cumber himself with prisoners.

61. Troops that give no quarter have no right to kill enemies already disabled on the ground, or prisoners captured by other troops.

62. All troops of the enemy known or discovered to give no quarter in general, or to any portion of the Army, receive none.

63. Troops who fight in the uniform of their enemies, without any plain, striking, and uniform mark of distinction of their own, can expect no quarter.

64. If American troops capture a train containing uniforms of the enemy, and the commander considers it advisable to distribute them for use among his men, some striking mark or sign must be adopted to distinguish the American soldier from the enemy.

65. The use of the enemy's national standard, flag, or other emblem of nationality, for the purpose of deceiving the enemy in battle, is an act of perfidy by which they lose all claim to the protection of the laws of war.

66. Quarter having been given to an enemy by American troops, under a misapprehension of his true character, he may, nevertheless, be ordered to suffer death if, within three days after the battle, it be discovered that he belongs to a corps which gives no quarter.

67. The law of nations allows every sovereign government to make war upon another sovereign State, and, therefore, admits of no rules or laws different from those of regular warfare, regarding the treatment of prisoners of war, although they may belong to the army of a government which the captor may consider as a wanton and unjust assailant.

68. Modern wars are not internecine wars, in which the killing of the enemy is the object. The destruction of the enemy in modern war, and, indeed, modern war itself, are means to obtain that object of the belligerent which lies beyond the war.

Unnecessary or revengeful destruction of life is not lawful.

69. Outposts, sentinels, or pickets are not to be fired upon, except to drive them in, or when a positive order, special or general, has been issued to that effect.

70. The use of poison in any manner, be it to poison wells, or food, or arms, is wholly excluded from modern warfare. He that uses it puts himself out of the pale of the law and usages of war.

71. Whoever intentionally inflicts additional wounds on an enemy already wholly disabled, or kills such an enemy, or who orders or encourages soldiers to do so, shall suffer death, if duly convicted, whether he belongs to the Army of the United States, or is an enemy captured after having committed his misdeed.

72. Money and other valuables on the person of a prisoner, such as watches or jewelry, as well as extra clothing, are regarded by the American Army as the private property of the prisoner, and the appropriation of such valuables or money is considered dishonorable, and is prohibited.

Nevertheless, if large sums are found upon the persons of prisoners, or in their possession, they shall be taken from them, and the surplus, after providing for their own support, appropriated for the use of the Army, under the direction of the commander, unless otherwise ordered by the Government. Nor can prisoners claim, as private property, large sums found and captured in their train, although they have been placed in the private luggage of the prisoners.

73. All officers, when captured, must surrender their side-arms to the captor. They may be restored to the prisoner in marked cases, by the commander, to signalize admiration of his distinguished bravery, or approbation of his humane treatment of prisoners before his capture. The captured officer to whom they may be restored cannot wear them during captivity.

74. A prisoner of war, being a public enemy, is the prisoner of the Government and not of the captor. No ransom can be paid by a prisoner of war to his individual captor, or to any officer in command. The Government alone releases captives, according to rules prescribed by itself.

75. Prisoners of war are subject to confinement or imprisonment such as may be deemed necessary on account of safety, but they are to be subjected to no other intentional suffering or indignity. The confinement and mode of treating a prisoner may be varied during his captivity according to the demands of safety.

76. Prisoners of war shall be fed upon plain and wholesome food, whenever practicable, and treated with humanity.

They may be required to work for the benefit of the captor's government, according to their rank and condition.

77. A prisoner of war who escapes may be shot, or otherwise killed, in his flight; but neither death nor any other punishment shall be inflicted upon him simply for his attempt to escape, which the law of war does not consider a crime. Stricter means of security shall be used after an unsuccessful attempt at escape.

If, however, a conspiracy is discovered, the purpose of which is a united or general escape, the conspirators may be rigorously punished, even with death; and capital punishment may also be inflicted upon prisoners of war discovered to have plotted rebellion against the authorities of the captors, whether in union with fellow-prisoners or other persons.

78. If prisoners of war, having given no pledge nor made any promise on their honor, forcibly or otherwise escape, and are captured again in battle, after having rejoined their own army, they shall not be punished for their escape, but shall be treated as simple prisoners of war, although they will be subjected to stricter confinement.

79. Every captured wounded enemy shall be medically treated, according to the ability of the medical staff.

80. Honorable men, when captured, will abstain from giving to the enemy information concerning their own army, and the modern law of war permits no longer the use of any violence

against prisoners in order to extort the desired information, or to punish them for having given false information.

SECTION IV.—*Partisans—Armed enemies not belonging to the hostile army—Scouts—Armed prowlers—War-rebels.*

81. Partisans are soldiers armed and wearing the uniform of their army, but belonging to a corps which acts detached from the main body for the purpose of making inroads into the territory occupied by the enemy. If captured they are entitled to all the privileges of the prisoner of war.

82. Men, or squads of men, who commit hostilities, whether by fighting, or inroads for destruction or plunder, or by raids of any kind, without commission, without being part and portion of the organized hostile army, and without sharing continuously in the war, but who do so with intermitting returns to their homes and avocations, or with the occasional assumption of the semblance of peaceful pursuits, divesting themselves of the character or appearance of soldiers—such men, or squads of men, are not public enemies, and therefore, if captured, are not entitled to the privileges of prisoners of war, but shall be treated summarily as highway robbers or pirates.

83. Scouts or single soldiers, if disguised in the dress of the country, or in the uniform of the army hostile to their own, employed in obtaining information, if found within or lurking about the lines of the captor, are treated as spies, and suffer death.

84. Armed prowlers, by whatever names they may be called, or persons of the enemy's territory, who steal within the lines of the hostile army for the purpose of robbing, killing, or of destroying bridges, roads, or canals, or of robbing or destroying the mail, or of cutting the telegraph wires, are not entitled to the privileges of the prisoner of war.

85. War-rebels are persons within an occupied territory who rise in arms against the occupying or conquering army, or against the authorities established by the same. If captured, they may suffer death, whether they rise singly, in small or large bands, and whether called upon to do so by their own, but expelled,

government or not. They are not prisoners of war; nor are they if discovered and secured before their conspiracy has matured to an actual rising or to armed violence.

SECTION V.—*Safe-conduct—Spies—War-traitors—Captured messengers—Abuse of the flag of truce.*

86. All intercourse between the territories occupied by belligerent armies, whether by traffic, by letter, by travel, or in any other way, ceases. This is the general rule, to be observed without special proclamation.

Exceptions to this rule, whether by safe-conduct or permission to trade on a small or large scale, or by exchanging mails, or by travel from one territory into the other, can take place only according to agreement approved by the Government or by the highest military authority.

Contraventions of this rule are highly punishable.

87. Ambassadors, and all other diplomatic agents of neutral powers accredited to the enemy may receive safe-conducts through the territories occupied by the belligerents, unless there are military reasons to the contrary, and unless they may reach the place of their destination conveniently by another route. It implies no international affront if the safe-conduct is declined. Such passes are usually given by the supreme authority of the state and not by subordinate officers.

88. A spy is a person who secretly, in disguise or under false pretense, seeks information with the intention of communicating it to the enemy.

The spy is punishable with death by hanging by the neck, whether or not he succeed in obtaining the information or in conveying it to the enemy.

89. If a citizen of the United States obtains information in a legitimate manner and betrays it to the enemy, be he a military or civil officer, or a private citizen, he shall suffer death.

90. A traitor under the law of war, or a war-traitor, is a person in a place or district under martial law who, unauthorized by the military commander, gives information of any kind to the enemy, or holds intercourse with him.

91. The war-traitor is always severely punished. If his offense consists in betraying to the enemy anything concerning the condition, safety, operations, or plans of the troops holding or occupying the place or district, his punishment is death.

92. If the citizen or subject of a country or place invaded or conquered gives information to his own government, from which he is separated by the hostile army, or to the army of his government, he is a war-traitor, and death is the penalty of his offense.

93. All armies in the field stand in need of guides, and impress them if they cannot obtain them otherwise.

94. No person having been forced by the enemy to serve as a guide is punishable for having done so.

95. If a citizen of a hostile and invaded district voluntarily serves as a guide to the enemy, or offers to do so, he is deemed a war-traitor and shall suffer death.

96. A citizen serving voluntarily as a guide against his own country commits treason, and will be dealt with according to the law of his country.

97. Guides, when it is clearly proved that they have misled intentionally, may be put to death.

98. All unauthorized or secret communication with the enemy is considered treasonable by the law of war.

Foreign residents in an invaded or occupied territory or foreign visitors in the same can claim no immunity from this law. They may communicate with foreign parts or with the inhabitants of the hostile country, so far as the military authority permits, but no further. Instant expulsion from the occupied territory would be the very least punishment for the infraction of this rule.

99. A messenger carrying written dispatches or verbal messages from one portion of the army or from a besieged place to another portion of the same army or its government, if armed, and in the uniform of his army, and if captured while doing so in the territory occupied by the enemy, is treated by the captor as a prisoner of war. If not in uniform nor a soldier, the circumstances connected with his capture must determine the disposition that shall be made of him.

100. A messenger or agent who attempts to steal through the territory occupied by the enemy to further in any manner the interests of the enemy, if captured, is not entitled to the privileges of the prisoner of war, and may be dealt with according to the circumstances of the case.

101. While deception in war is admitted as a just and necessary means of hostility, and is consistent with honorable warfare, the common law of war allows even capital punishment for clandestine or treacherous attempts to injure an enemy, because they are so dangerous, and it is so difficult to guard against them.

102. The law of war, like the criminal law regarding other offenses, makes no difference on account of the difference of sexes, concerning the spy, the war-traitor, or the war-rebel.

103. Spies, war-traitors, and war-rebels are not exchanged according to the common law of war. The exchange of such persons would require a special cartel, authorized by the Government, or, at a great distance from it, by the chief commander of the army in the field.

104. A successful spy or war-traitor, safely returned to his own army, and afterward captured as an enemy, is not subject to punishment for his acts as a spy or war-traitor, but he may be held in closer custody as a person individually dangerous.

SECTION VI.—*Exchange of prisoners—Flags of truce—Flags of protection.*

105. Exchanges of prisoners take place—number for number—rank for rank—wounded for wounded—with added condition for added condition—such, for instance, as not to serve for a certain period.

106. In exchanging prisoners of war, such numbers of persons of inferior rank may be substituted as an equivalent for one of superior rank as may be agreed upon by cartel, which requires the sanction of the Government, or of the commander of the army in the field.

107. A prisoner of war is in honor bound truly to state to the captor his rank; and he is not to assume a lower rank than belongs

to him, in order to cause a more advantageous exchange, nor a higher rank, for the purpose of obtaining better treatment.

Offenses to the contrary have been justly punished by the commanders of released prisoners, and may be good cause for refusing to release such prisoners.

108. The surplus number of prisoners of war remaining after an exchange has taken place is sometimes released either for the payment of a stipulated sum of money, or, in urgent cases, of provision, clothing, or other necessaries.

Such arrangement, however, requires the sanction of the highest authority.

109. The exchange of prisoners of war is an act of convenience to both belligerents. If no general cartel has been concluded, it cannot be demanded by either of them. No belligerent is obliged to exchange prisoners of war.

A cartel is voidable as soon as either party has violated it.

110. No exchange of prisoners shall be made except after complete capture, and after an accurate account of them, and a list of the captured officers, has been taken.

111. The bearer of a flag of truce cannot insist upon being admitted. He must always be admitted with great caution. Unnecessary frequency is carefully to be avoided.

112. If the bearer of a flag of truce offer himself during an engagement, he can be admitted as a very rare exception only. It is no breach of good faith to retain such flag of truce, if admitted during the engagement. Firing is not required to cease on the appearance of a flag of truce in battle.

113. If the bearer of a flag of truce, presenting himself during an engagement, is killed or wounded, it furnishes no ground of complaint whatever.

114. If it be discovered, and fairly proved, that a flag of truce has been abused for surreptitiously obtaining military knowledge, the bearer of the flag thus abusing his sacred character is deemed a spy.

So sacred is the character of a flag of truce, and so necessary is its sacredness, that while its abuse is an especially heinous offense, great caution is requisite, on the other hand, in convicting the bearer of a flag of truce as a spy.

115. It is customary to designate by certain flags (usually yellow) the hospitals in places which are shelled, so that the besieging enemy may avoid firing on them. The same has been done in battles when hospitals are situated within the field of the engagement.

116. Honorable belligerents often request that the hospitals within the territory of the enemy may be designated, so that they may be spared.

An honorable belligerent allows himself to be guided by flags or signals of protection as much as the contingencies and the necessities of the fight will permit.

117. It is justly considered an act of bad faith, of infamy or fiendishness, to deceive the enemy by flags of protection. Such act of bad faith may be good cause for refusing to respect such flags.

118. The besieging belligerent has sometimes requested the besieged to designate the buildings containing collections of works of art, scientific museums, astronomical observatories, or precious libraries, so that their destruction may be avoided as much as possible.

SECTION VII.—*The parole.*

119. Prisoners of war may be released from captivity by exchange, and, under certain circumstances, also by parole.

120. The term parole designates the pledge of individual good faith and honor to do, or to omit doing, certain acts after he who gives his parole shall have been dismissed, wholly or partially, from the power of the captor.

121. The pledge of the parole is always an individual, but not a private act.

122. The parole applies chiefly to prisoners of war whom the captor allows to return to their country, or to live in greater freedom within the captor's country or territory, on conditions stated in the parole.

123. Release of prisoners of war by exchange is the general rule; release by parole is the exception.

124. Breaking the parole is punished with death when the person breaking the parole is captured again.

Accurate lists, therefore, of the paroled persons must be kept by the belligerents.

125. When paroles are given and received there must be an exchange of two written documents, in which the name and rank of the paroled individuals are accurately and truthfully stated.

126. Commissioned officers only are allowed to give their parole, and they can give it only with the permission of their superior, as long as a superior rank is within reach.

127. No non-commissioned officer or private can give his parole except through an officer. Individual paroles not given through an officer are not only void, but subject the individuals giving them to the punishment of death as deserters. The only admissible exception is where individuals, properly separated from their commands, have suffered long confinement without the possibility of being paroled through an officer.

128. No paroling on the battle-field; no paroling of entire bodies of troops after a battle; and no dismissal of large numbers of prisoners, with a general declaration that they are paroled, is permitted, or of any value.

129. In capitulations for the surrender of strong places or fortified camps the commanding officer, in cases of urgent necessity, may agree that the troops under his command shall not fight again during the war unless exchanged.

130. The usual pledge given in the parole is not to serve during the existing war unless exchanged.

This pledge refers only to the active service in the field against the paroling belligerent or his allies actively engaged in the same war. These cases of breaking the parole are patent acts, and can be visited with the punishment of death; but the pledge does not refer to internal service, such as recruiting or drilling the recruits, fortifying places not besieged, quelling civil commotions, fighting against belligerents unconnected with the paroling belligerents, or to civil or diplomatic service for which the paroled officer may be employed.

131. If the government does not approve of the parole, the paroled officer must return into captivity, and should the enemy refuse to receive him he is free of his parole.

132. A belligerent government may declare, by a general order, whether it will allow paroling and on what conditions it will allow it. Such order is communicated to the enemy.

133. No prisoner of war can be forced by the hostile government to parole himself, and no government is obliged to parole prisoners of war or to parole all captured officers, if it paroles any. As the pledging of the parole is an individual act, so is paroling, on the other hand, an act of choice on the part of the belligerent.

134. The commander of an occupying army may require of the civil officers of the enemy, and of its citizens, any pledge he may consider necessary for the safety or security of his army, and upon their failure to give it he may arrest, confine, or detain them.

SECTION VIII.—*Armistice—Capitulation.*

135. An armistice is the cessation of active hostilities for a period agreed between belligerents. It must be agreed upon in writing and duly ratified by the highest authorities of the contending parties.

136. If an armistice be declared without conditions it extends no further than to require a total cessation of hostilities along the front of both belligerents.

If conditions be agreed upon, they should be clearly expressed, and must be rigidly adhered to by both parties. If either party violates any express condition, the armistice may be declared null and void by the other.

137. An armistice may be general, and valid for all points and lines of the belligerents; or special—that is, referring to certain troops or certain localities only.

An armistice may be concluded for a definite time; or for an indefinite time, during which either belligerent may resume hostilities on giving the notice agreed upon to the other.

138. The motives which induce the one or the other belligerent to conclude an armistice, whether it be expected to be preliminary to a treaty of peace, or to prepare during the armistice for a more vigorous prosecution of the war, does in no way affect the character of the armistice itself.

139. An armistice is binding upon the belligerents from the day of the agreed commencement; but the officers of the armies are responsible from the day only when they receive official information of its existence.

140. Commanding officers have the right to conclude armistices binding on the district over which their command extends, but such armistice is subject to the ratification of the superior authority, and ceases so soon as it is made known to the enemy that the armistice is not ratified, even if a certain time for the elapsing between giving notice of cessation and the resumption of hostilities should have been stipulated for.

141. It is incumbent upon the contracting parties of an armistice to stipulate what intercourse of persons or traffic between the inhabitants of the territories occupied by the hostile armies shall be allowed, if any.

If nothing is stipulated the intercourse remains suspended, as during actual hostilities.

142. An armistice is not a partial or a temporary peace; it is only the suspension of military operations to the extent agreed upon by the parties.

143. When an armistice is concluded between a fortified place and the army besieging it, it is agreed by all the authorities on this subject that the besieger must cease all extension, perfection, or advance of his attacking works as much so as from attacks by main force.

But as there is a difference of opinion among martial jurists whether the besieged have a right to repair breaches or to erect new works of defense within the place during an armistice, this point should be determined by express agreement between the parties.

144. So soon as a capitulation is signed the capitulator has no right to demolish, destroy, or injure the works, arms, stores, or ammunition in his possession, during the time which elapses between the signing and the execution of the capitulation, unless otherwise stipulated in the same.

145. When an armistice is clearly broken by one of the parties the other party is released from all obligation to observe it.

146. Prisoners taken in the act of breaking an armistice must be treated as prisoners of war, the officer alone being responsible who gives the order for such a violation of an armistice. The highest authority of the belligerent aggrieved may demand redress for the infraction of an armistice.

147. Belligerents sometimes conclude an armistice while their plenipotentiaries are met to discuss the conditions of a treaty of peace; but plenipotentiaries may meet without a preliminary armistice; in the latter case the war is carried on without any abatement.

SECTION IX.—*Assassination.*

148. The law of war does not allow proclaiming either an individual belonging to the hostile army, or a citizen, or a subject of the hostile government an outlaw, who may be slain without trial by any captor, any more than the modern law of peace allows such international outlawry; on the contrary, it abhors such outrage. The sternest retaliation should follow the murder committed in consequence of such proclamation, made by whatever authority. Civilized nations look with horror upon offers of rewards for the assassination of enemies as relapses into barbarism.

SECTION X.—*Insurrection—Civil war—Rebellion.*

149. Insurrection is the rising of people in arms against their government, or a portion of it, or against one or more of its laws, or against an officer or officers of the government. It may be confined to mere armed resistance, or it may have greater ends in view.

150. Civil war is war between two or more portions of a country or state, each contending for the mastery of the whole, and each claiming to be the legitimate government. The term is also sometimes applied to war of rebellion, when the rebellious provinces or portions of the state are contiguous to those containing the seat of government.

151. The term rebellion is applied to an insurrection of large extent, and is usually a war between the legitimate government of a country and portions or provinces of the same who seek to throw off their allegiance to it and set up a government of their own.

152. When humanity induces the adoption of the rules of regular war toward rebels, whether the adoption is partial or entire, it does in no way whatever imply a partial or complete acknowledgment of their government, if they have set up one, or of them, as an independent or sovereign power. Neutrals have no right to make the adoption of the rules of war by the assailed government toward rebels the ground of their own acknowledgment of the revolted people as an independent power.

153. Treating captured rebels as prisoners of war, exchanging them, concluding of cartels, capitulations, or other warlike agreements with them; addressing officers of a rebel army by the rank they may have in the same; accepting flags of truce; or, on the other hand, proclaiming martial law in their territory, or levying war taxes or forced loans, or doing any other act sanctioned or demanded by the law and usages of public war between sovereign belligerents, neither proves nor establishes an acknowledgment of the rebellious people, or of the government which they may have erected, as a public or sovereign power. Nor does the adoption of the rules of war toward rebels imply an engagement with them extending beyond the limits of these rules. It is victory in the field that ends the strife and settles the future relations between the contending parties.

154. Treating in the field the rebellious enemy according to the law and usages of war has never prevented the legitimate government from trying the leaders of the rebellion or chief rebels

for high treason, and from treating them accordingly, unless they are included in a general amnesty.

155. All enemies in regular war are divided into two general classes—that is to say, into combatants and non-combatants, or unarmed citizens of the hostile government.

The military commander of the legitimate government, in a war of rebellion, distinguishes between the loyal citizen in the revolted portion of the country and the disloyal citizen. The disloyal citizens may further be classified into those citizens known to sympathize with the rebellion without positively aiding it, and those who, without taking up arms, give positive aid and comfort to the rebellious enemy without being bodily forced thereto.

156. Common justice and plain expediency require that the military commander protect the manifestly loyal citizens in revolted territories against the hardships of the war as much as the common misfortune of all war admits.

The commander will throw the burden of the war, as much as lies within his power, on the disloyal citizens, of the revolted portion or province, subjecting them to a stricter police than the non-combatant enemies have to suffer in regular war; and if he deems it appropriate, or if his government demands of him that every citizen shall, by an oath of allegiance, or by some other manifest act, declare his fidelity to the legitimate government, he may expel, transfer, imprison, or fine the revolted citizens who refuse to pledge themselves anew as citizens obedient to the law and loyal to the government.

Whether it is expedient to do so, and whether reliance can be placed upon such oaths, the commander or his government have the right to decide.

157. Armed or unarmed resistance by citizens of the United States against the lawful movements of their troops is levying war against the United States, and is therefore treason.

III Selected Correspondence and Documents

Francis Lieber was a prolific correspondent. The bulk of his surviving letters is available, with other manuscripts, at the Henry E. Huntington Library, San Marino, California. Some have been reprinted, more or less accurately, in studies dealing with the broad range of Lieber's thought. The letters presented here, in chronological order, are from two sources: the Huntington collection (indicated by citation as *HL*) and the official government records, *The War of the Rebellion: A Compilation of the Official Records of the Union and Confederate Armies* (indicated by citation as *WR*).

Selection of these letters was determined by their pertinence to the documents reprinted in Parts I and II. The exchanges between Lieber and Halleck deal primarily with the initiation, compilation and completion of Lieber's essay on guerrilla warfare and the subsequent "General Orders, No. 100." The remaining official correspondence reveals attempts by Union and Confederate officials to apply these documents.

In most of the Lieber-Halleck correspondence, a second theme continually recurs: both men's concern for the progress and prosecution of the Civil War, and their apprehensiveness about what they detect, and detest, as the intrusion of subversive political machinations.

Finally, their letters implicitly reveal the personal qualities of both men: their deference and respect for each other as fellow scholars; an obvious friendship and warmth, decorated by the requisite nineteenth century formality; and Lieber's passionate concern for the well-being of two of his sons, Hamilton and Norman. A measure of his nationalist fervor, and perhaps private agony and personal hurt, is his failure to name his youngest son, the apostate Oscar, who had chosen to fight for the Confederacy, although he does allude to him.

If one theme dominates the correspondence between officials of the warring parties, it is the difficulty, for these men at war, of separating themselves as fellow human beings into the category of mutual enemies. Lieber's efforts at least offered some tentative limits to aid both parties toward a more humane prosecution of an ugly conflict.

I have reproduced these documents exactly, with no attempt to edit personal or nineteenth century usages, in the interest of preserving their spirit and nuances. Where misprints, misspellings or obvious omissions have occurred, their correction is bracketed.

Lieber, New York, to Halleck, Washington, 23 July, 1862 [HL].

Confidential
My dear General,

I just read in the evening paper of your high appointment. May our army profit under you and may victory once more return to us. It is even necessary for our very enlistments. The state of things in fact now here [is] very bad. If you desire I can give you some elements of a correct opinion; I would even go to Washington, did I know I could have an undisturbed conversation, or rather exchange of thought with you. The Germans here flatly decline enlisting, despite the high bounty. What should we do it for, they say—to be dragged about for nothing?

You wrote to me once from the West to send you my lectures on the Law of War, or a syllabus of them. They were not printed. I enclose a copy of my letter to the Attorney General on a question which I know will interest you as jurist and soldier. Grant me the favor of a perusal.

I am now studying for myself the very important question of *Guerrilleros*.

I ought to add that as soon as my letter to the Attorney General was published (not without his permission), I wrote to Mrs. Halleck to give me your address because I desired to send it to you. She was out of town and received my note but very recently, after I had seen indications of your being placed in the position you now hold, and in which I pray God he may give you the wisest counsel and the most vivid energy. . . .

The arm of my son, Hamilton, is not right yet.

My son Norman (Adjutant of the Eleventh U.S. Infantry) passed safely through the week's battle. He had one horse shot, and one wounded but all these individual things must sound strangely to you on your high mountain peak of command and authority, so I will only add that, since I saw you I have had the very great pleasure—and it is more than that—of becoming acquainted with Mrs. Halleck. My wife fully shares in this pleasure.

I am most sincerely my dear General,

Your friend and servant
not your "half countryman" but your entire fellow American
Francis Lieber

Halleck, Washington, to Lieber, New York, 30 July, 1862 [HL].

My dear Doctor:

Yours of the 23d inst. is just received. I have attentively read your letter to Attorney General Bates. I fully endorse all you say in that letter. Our people and government are only beginning to understand martial law and its effects on municipal law and civil courts.

I am very anxious to see your views of guerrilla war, as I hear that you are writing on that subject. I treated it very briefly in my book, not expecting at that time that we should ever have guerrillas in the U. States. It has now become an important question in this country and should be thoroughly investigated. I know of no one who can do it as well as yourself.

A very stringent order will be published today in regard to absentees. Orders are also in preparation respecting recruiting and drafting. This is a terrible war and will require mighty efforts to terminate it. I hope the north will fully wake up to the necessity of more vigorous efforts.

When your son is sufficiently recovered to go on duty I shall want him here. When he reported at Corinth he was still suffering very much and I advised not to attempt doing duty till his wound was fully healed.

Yours in haste. . .

Lieber, New York, to Halleck, Washington, 1 August, 1862 [HL].

Private and Confidential
My dear General,

Your favour of the 30th July reached me yesterday evening. It gives me sincere pleasure that you express your entire agreement with my letter to the Attorney General Bates. Our war is abnormal in many respects, and its many and *deep* difficulties are proportionate, the more necessary it becomes to act both, with unsurpassed energy and with the utmost distinctness of purpose and clearness of thought. My notes concerning *guerrilleros* are nearly complete, and my thoughts on this topic are pretty clear and defined. It is now the question how to shape them, in what form to give them to the public. I would probably not like to give them again in the form of a letter to some person in high position. Can there be such a thing as being called upon by high authority, by you for instance, or Secretary Stanton to give my views? I shall see you, probably, on Monday or Tuesday next, and can converse with you on the subject when I can give you my chief and leading ideas so that you may readily see what the paper would be. In the meantime I beg to make this request, that one of your officers will get a copy ready (if printed, so much the better), 1. of your own order to shoot guerrilla men in Missouri, 2. the President's counter-order, and command not to shoot them. I shall probably go to Washington as one of a Committee sent by our convention of committees of sundry bodies of citizens of New York.

You say: "I hope the north will fully wake up to the necessity of more vigorous efforts." My dear General, this is a strictly confidential letter, and in such a one I cannot see that there can be any objection to my saying that all along the universal feeling of the loyal men has been that they are ready for any effort—they have longed for vigour and decision, they have felt as though the government was not sufficiently in full earnest. They have yearned for concentrated blows, physical and moral, and government has directed a scattered pelting. Right or wrong, I merely speak of the fact of this feeling. As to the present moment there is a general feeling not of despondency—but of weary depression and of great alacrity in the treasonable ones, of whom we have many in the midst of us. Take it also as a fact that no very long extension of this state of things is necessary to produce an open re-organization of treason in this city under the form of peace meetings. If this sounds startling to you, it is nevertheless true. Action and success alone can weigh down again this intramural treason.

The end of your favour refers to my brave Hamilton. There seems to be a misunderstanding. He never complains, but in his last letter from near Corinth (he is with his regiment, 9th Illinois Infantry) he says that his arm has troubled him much, and that he has sent in his resignation, for the acceptance of which he waited. I have written at once to him to offer his services to the Govern. of Illinois, in the recruiting business. I thank you for your intention to have him with you in Washington. God grant the amputation, which I know was made bunglingly, will not require a second one! Nor would, I believe, his proper sphere be on a Washington staff. But I have a son in the army, who would be highly useful on your staff, and to him I could wish you could transfer your kind consideration. My youngest son, G. Norman Lieber, 1st Lieut. and regimental adjutant in the Eleventh U.S. Regular Infantry, is 25 years old, of military stature, has not had a day's sickness in the whole campaign. He received his commission in April (I think) 1861, and has been adjutant ever since, to the full satisfaction of his commander, Lt. Col. Shriver (now, I believe on the staff of Genl. McDowell) and Major Jones, now commanding the 11th U.S. Infantry. Norman passed through the week's battle near Richmond; had his horse killed, and another wounded, but so far he has been more lucky than his father and two brothers. He graduated with distinction, studied law and was a lawyer until commissioned. He has ever been an assiduous student, is a ready writer, and dutiful in every respect. I doubt not in the least that he is gallant. His commander has spoken well of him in the regimental report to Genl. McClellan. He never complains, and I conscientiously believe him to be an excellent soldier and good officer. Does he fit for some place that you may have?

With sincere friendship, my dear General

Your
Francis Lieber

Halleck, Washington, to Lieber, New York, 6 August, 1862 [HL], and [WR], ser. III, vol. II, 301.

My dear Doctor:

Hearing that you have given much attention to the usages and customs of war as practiced in the present age, and especially to the matter of guerrilla war, I hope you may find it convenient to give to the public your views on that subject. The Rebel authorities claim the right to send men in the garb of peaceful citizens to waylay and attack our troops, to burn bridges and houses, and to destroy property and persons within our lines. They demand that such persons be treated as ordinary belligerents, and that when captured they have extended to them the same rights as other prisoners of war; they also threaten that if such persons be punished as marauders and spies they will retaliate by executing our prisoners of war in their possession.

I particularly request your views on these questions.

Very respectfully. . . .
Your obedient servant

Halleck, Washington, to Lieber, New York, 20 August, 1862 [HL].

My dear Dr.

I have hastily read your essay and highly approve it. I return it herewith, with an order for 5,000 copies.

I recommend you to Van Nostrand, Publisher, No. 172 Broadway. He has facilities for giving sale to books etc. on military subjects and probably could sell a thousand or two additional copies.

Your son G. N. has been appointed Aide de Camp.

Yours in haste. . .

Lieber, New York, to Halleck, Washington, 13 November, 1862 [HL].

My dear General,

Please reflect on the accompanying letter and decide whether anything of the kind proposed in it, can be . . . of importance. . . .

I trust to Heaven that the idea of an armistice, which is making its appearance in the party, which has carried, of late, the elections, is not entertained in high quarters. It would be the certain precursor of separation; and separation would be the precursor of ruin—the survival of a Medieval state of things, an unavoidable downward course.

But I must not detain you. Of course the accompanying letter can be shown, if you think fit, to whomever you choose.

Lieber, New York, to Halleck, Washington, 13 November, 1862 [HL].

My dear General,

Ever since the beginning of our present War, it has appeared clearer and clearer to me, that the President ought to issue a set of rules and definitions providing for the most urgent issues occurring under the Law and usages of War, and on which our Articles of War are silent. The last phases of our war, and the things which have come to light by the recent inquiries into the conduct of certain officers, have at length induced me to write to you on the subject. I address you as the jurist, no less than as the soldier.

My idea is—I give it as a suggestion to you—that the President as Commander in Chief, through the Secretary of War, ought to appoint a committee, say of three, to draw up a code, if you choose to call it so, in which certain acts and offences (under the Law of War) ought to be defined and, where necessary, the punishment be stated.

For instance:

The Spy—Who is a spy? How is the spy to be punished?

Paroling—What is it? Who paroles? What punishment for breaking the parole?

Who shall be treated as prisoner of war? etc, etc, etc.

I do not know that any such thing as I design exists in any other country, and in all other countries the Law of War is much more reduced to naked Force or Might, than we are willing to do it, especially now, perhaps, in this Civil War, and there exists much more thorough organization in those countries; nor do single wars extend there over such distances as here.

If the President believes that he has not the authority to proclaim such a set of rules, then it ought to be done by the help of Congress.

I should propose that you, both as General-in-Chief and as a prominent writer on the Law of Nations, ought to be chairman of this important Committee, to supervise the general laying out of the plan and for the ultimate revising of the whole. I know full well how much your time is occupied, but this business seems to me as important as any other that can now occupy the minds of men in highest positions.

The mail between New York and Washington is in such a disorder that I shall consider it as a favour if you will direct some one to inform me of the receipt of this note.

I am with the highest regard. . .

Lieber's private notes on his letter to Halleck

In answer to a letter in which I asked Genl. Halleck to induce the President to appoint a Committee to draw up a code, as it were concerning the Law of War so far as it relates to the intercourse of . . . actual belligerents, and as it is not touched upon in our Articles of War (esp., Paroling, Capitulation, Prisoner of War, etc. etc.); and in which I said that if the President cannot act alone, that such a code (very brief indeed . . .) should nevertheless be drawn up and an attempt be made to get it sanctioned by Congress.

F.L.

Halleck, Washington, to Lieber, New York, 15 November, 1862 [HL].

My dear Doctor,

Yours of the 13th is received. I have no time at present to consider the subject mentioned in the paper enclosed.

No fear of an "armistice." The matter will not be considered for a moment. If the states would only supply the troops asked for last August, the rebellion would soon receive its death blow. But all our plans are thwarted by the want of troops. We scarcely receive enough to compensate for wastage.

Yours truly. . .

Lieber, New York, to Halleck, Washington, 20 November, 1862 [HL].

Private
My dear General,

I dare say that in the peculiar American division of public labour—I shall rather say, overwhelming concentration of labour, you cannot find time to reflect on a proposition such as I lately made to you. I shall not make it to the Secretary of War, or to the President; for I think it is you from whom the movement ought to have proceeded. I am sorry; for, the more I reflect on the matter, the more important it appears to me.

Thank you for what you write to me about an armistice. It has been stated to me that some persons highest among those who have succeeded in the last New York election, the idea of sending a secret agent to Richmond is now discussing *[sic]*. Quite likely, similar things have happened in similar periods of history.

What you write about the failure of troops, and indeed, what happens around us regarding the draft, is distressing. The serious mistake, it seems to me, has been that the first draft was not limited to the age from 20 to 25 or to 30. If Government could not act otherwise, being banned by Law, which I do not know, it was and is a serious evil and not a mistake.

I fear very serious consequences from the election of Gov. Seymour. Perhaps you know him personally, and think my fears are unfounded. May God grant that it be so.

I found the following passage in a letter written by Washington to Col. Laurens in 1782: "That spirit of freedom which, at the commencement of this contest, would have gladly sacrificed everything to the attainment of its object, has long since subsided, and every selfish passion has taken its place." *Mutatus mutandis* this applies to us now. There was a great *elan* at the beginning of this contest, but no great man in Washington to utilize it.

Still, Washington was tenacious . . . and he succeeded. Be you, my dear Friend, tenacious like him, like William the Silent. Would to God, I could say: I will do all in my power to aid and second you! But I and Doing are two different things. A profession in a College, and doing anything in this great struggle! It is this that makes this period so very sad to me.

Ever very truly,
Your friend and servant. . .

Halleck, Washington, to Lieber, New York, 23 November, 1862 [HL].

My dear Dr.

Yours of the 20th is received. I have hardly time to acknowledge it. The matter of your former letter cannot be taken up at present, as every officer of rank here, in addition to his arduous duties connected with the war, is preparing estimates, reports, etc. for Congress. Until this is done no one will have a moment to spare for other things.

I agree with you in your fears of state difficulties. I warned the government months ago that by deferring every thing to Governors of States, it was building up a northern states rights party that would eventually overpower all Federal authority. No heed has been given to the warning, but approaching danger is already visible.

There is in this administration, or rather I should say in the cabinet, a power of weakness—a courage of timidity, that attempts everything and yet does nothing. Not satisfied with having so many irons in the fire that nearly all burn, new ones must be thrust in daily. I really almost begin to doubt the good faith of this spasmodic but marplot energy. Has it been the object of those men to whom I refer to prosecute a real bona-fide war? Are they not playing a political game? Is there not some great political plot with its headquarters in New York, to prolong the war by preventing any decisive result? I sometimes almost think so. I hope, however, that everything may go right, even in New York.

Yours truly. . .

Lieber, New York, to Halleck, Washington, 25 November, 1862 [HL].

Private and Confidential

Yes, yes indeed, my dear General, you are right, I believe in every line you wrote me.

I, as a native German who longed for the Unity of his country from his very boyhood cannot be expected to lean much toward State Rights doctrine *North* or South. With all my abhorrence of French Centralism, I always boldly assert, as political philosopher, the inherent weakness of Confederate Government.

I have just delivered in the Law School three entire lectures on the fact that the National type is the *normal* type of government of our race in modern times.

The present governor of S. Carolina delivered in my presence a speech in favour of the German Empire and of its present political organization. "May Heaven help you," I thought, "You are a dunce."

As to my *Committee* I submit, fully and frankly. But I hope you will take the suggestion out of the pigeon hole of your mind . . . .

In the meantime I mean to elaborate the chapter in *Paroling* by way of sample. Never was a thing in a more deplorable confusion and at the same time in a more disastrous state of expansion as that very Paroling in the present state of our war.

You wrote me a word of comfort some time ago concerning *armistice;* May God grant something similar may be said concerning that cloud which is rising on the horizon called intervention.

Ever your friend. . .

Lieber, New York, to Halleck, Washington, 7 December, 1862 [HL].

My dear General,

This moment I received your telegraph of yesterday. I shall start immediately after church (I cannot find any one at an earlier time) to see the chairman of the Board of Trustees of the College. In the meantime I would ask you whether it would not be well to telegraph to Hon. Hamilton Fish, Stuyvesant Square, New York, to ask of him to let me go, if the business for which I seem to be wanted is of sufficient importance. Hamilton Fish is chairman of the Board of Trustees, and, as you know, I cannot leave the College and Law School, now, when both are in full block, without losing my place, unless the Trustees give permission. . . .

Somehow people seem to *feel better.* Why? No matter now; the fact seems to me to be decidedly so.

Ever yours *very* truly. . .

Lieber, New York, to Halleck, Washington, 7 December, 1862 [HL].

My dear General,

I have this moment sent a telegraph to you, begging you to telegraph to the Hon. Hamilton Fish, Stuyvesant Square, New York . . . He is Chairman of the Board of Trustees of Columbia College. Very possibly this sheet may reach you before the telegraph. It is for this reason that I write this note in the office. There is no other paper here. I have already taken a letter addressed to you to the post office.

Very truly yours,

Lieber, New York, to Halleck, Washington, 9 December, 1862 [HL].

My dear General,

The Trustees have very promptly given leave to me to go to Washington as long as January 2nd. I shall be free to leave New York on Friday. Not knowing for what my presence is wanted

I cannot know whether this will suit the Secretary of War. I thought a letter explanatory in some way, or the telegraph would follow it, but nothing except the telegraph of Saturday which reached me Sunday morning has come to me.

With sincere friendship and the highest regard

Your obedient servant . . .

The official orders establishing Lieber's committee. [WR, ser. III, vol. II, 951] 17 December 1862.

SPECIAL ORDERS, No. 399. WAR DEPT., ADJT. GENERAL'S OFFICE, *Washington, December 17, 1862.*

* * * * * * *

5. Francis Lieber, L.L. D.; Maj. Gen. E. A. Hitchcock, U.S. Volunteers; Maj. Gen. G. Cadwalader, U.S. Volunteers; Maj. Gen. George L. Hartsuff, U.S. Volunteers, and Brig. Gen. J. H. Martindale, U.S. Volunteers, will constitute a board to propose amendments or changes in the Rules and Articles of War, and a code of regulations for the government of armies in the field, as authorized by the laws and usages of war.

The Board will meet in the city of Washington at such times as the members may agree upon.

* * * * * * *

By order of the Secretary of War:

E. D. TOWNSEND,
Assistant Adjutant-General.

Communique to President Lincoln from citizens in the Missouri Territory, expressing their concern over guerrilla activity. [WR, ser. I, vol. XXII, Part II, 3–5], 1 January 1863.

HEADQUARTERS DEPARTMENT OF THE MISSOURI,
Saint Louis, January 1, 1863.

Col. J. C. KELTON,
Assistant Adjutant-General, Washington, D.C.:

I have the honor to send herewith copy of my reply to Major-General Holmes' letter of the 7th ultimo, in which, by direction of his commander-in-chief, he asks full information in regard to the execution of ten men, by order of Brigadier-General McNeil, Missouri State Militia, some time since in Northeastern Missouri.

The question is one of some delicacy, and I hope my solution of it will meet the approval of the General-in-Chief.

I am, colonel, very respectfully, your obedient servant,

SAML. R. CURTIS,
Major-General.

NORTHERN MISSOURI, *January 1, 1863.*

His Excellency ABRAHAM LINCOLN,
President of the United States:

Your memorialists, loyal citizens of the United States and of the State of Missouri, respectfully represent that, since the outbreak of the present rebellion, Northern Missouri, in common with the southern part of the State, has been infested by hordes of lawless depredators, popularly known as guerrillas, though styling themselves "Confederate soldiers," led by desperate and unprincipled men, having not even the form of official commissions from the authorities of the so-called Confederate States, and whose modes of warfare have been only those resorted to and practiced by highway robbers, thieves, murderers, and assassins. Not having from any source a recognition as belligerents, they have, nevertheless, not scrupled to wage relentless war against the Government of the United States and of the State of Missouri, and against the peace, safety, and happiness of the loyal citizens of this State. In thus doing, they have causelessly murdered non-combatants by hanging, by shooting, by cutting their throats, and by divers other cruel, inhuman, and outrageous methods. They have fired into railroad trains, killing and maiming soldiers and citizens, and placing in imminent peril the lives of women and children. They have burned and destroyed railroad bridges, thereby causing trains filled with non-combatants to be precipitated into streams, killing, drowning, and wounding many persons, including women and children. They have, in the darkness of night, summoned citizens to the doors of their dwellings and there shot them dead. They have deliberately, and without provocation, fired into dwellings, placing in extreme jeopardy the lives of innocent and helpless persons therein. They have abducted citizens from their dwellings and families and murdered them secretly, and by methods unknown to the community at large. They have practiced inhuman and diabolical cruelties upon prisoners in their hands by brutally whipping and hanging them until nearly dead. And all this has been done for no other reason than that the parties thus murdered and outraged were, and had been, true and faithful in their allegiance to the United States. More than this, they have robbed the loyal citizens of Northern Missouri of hundreds of thousands of dollars' worth of property, taking in numerous instances the only horse from a needy and dependent family. They have stripped thousands of families of clothing, money, grain, cattle, wagons, arms, and ammunition, and, in short, of everything which their cupidity could lead them to covet or their wants to desire. Nor have these operations been confined to a few or remote localities. Every county, every community, has thus been scourged, until scarcely a loyal family has remained untouched. Thus these desperadoes desolated the whole land, establishing a reign of terror. Under this scourge many loyal citizens have fled from the State to preserve their lives; many have been forced to abandon their families and take refuge in the Federal army, and for weeks and months thousands have been nightly driven to the woods and fields to find shelter from the fury of these prowling fiends.

Your Excellency will not, however, understand that during all this time the United States and State Governments have been inactive in their efforts to crush out rebellion in this section of the State. Many thousand troops have occupied and held the various important points in Northern Missouri, and at no time have these guerrillas been able to withstand, in open conflict, by any combination of their forces, the regularly organized troops of the Government. But the character of their warfare and their intimacy with the topography of the country have been such that eighteen months' experience has demonstrated that organized troops, in however large bodies, simply holding isolated points, with ample power to control any given point, but governed only by the rules and methods of ordinary and regular warfare, could not check the outrages referred to, nor assure peace and safety to the loyal people. Experience long since convinced the military authorities of this department that something more was necessary than the mere occupancy of the country by Federal troops and the dispersion of aggregated bands of marauders. Hence the orders of Generals Halleck and Schofield, the point of which was that all guerrillas taken in arms should be shot. Had those orders in every instance been strictly carried out, it cannot be doubted that the effect would have been most happy. But too many such persons fell into the hands of our military authorities, who lacked the nerve to administer the required penalty. The result was thousands of these desperadoes were released on parole and bond; the country was again overrun by them, and their reiterated acts of brigandism were none the less violent or atrocious that they involved the additional crime of perjury. Oaths and bonds imposed no restraint upon such persons, whose demoniac passions now burned with a new and doubly heated flame.

It was in these dark days, when this whole section was in terror and dismay at the unchecked and apparently uncontrollable outrages of these men, that Brig. Gen. John McNeil, Missouri State Militia, commanding the Division of Northeastern Missouri, caused ten of these persons, all of whom had been, and at the time of their capture were, participants in the outrages of the general nature recited, to be publicly executed at Palmyra, in this State. The immediate occasion for this execution was the abduction and undoubted murder by these men, or their associates in crime, of one Andrew Allsman, a loyal citizen of Palmyra, a noncombatant, a man respectable in character and advanced in years. It was not, however, simply to avenge his death that ten criminals were executed. It was, additionally, to vindicate the power and authority of law and of the Government; to strike terror into the hearts of those whom no sentiments of right, honor, or justice could reach. It was to give safety and peace to this distracted country, and to assure the now almost incredulous people that the Government was not utterly powerless for their protection. It was a stroke absolutely essential to teach traitors that they could not, and should not, with impunity, outrage the rights and sacrifice the happiness and safety of whole communities. The act has achieved its desired purpose. The law and the supremacy of our Government are vindicated. Citizens return in peace and safety to their homes. They are no longer assassinated at pleasure by lawless ruffians. They feel that in truth they have a Government, and that that Government is, indeed, able and willing to cover them with its protecting shield.

Your memorialists have observed with many apprehensions the demand made by Jefferson Davis, President of the so-called Confederate States, for the delivery of General McNeil to the Confederate authorities. We therefore adopt this method and take this occasion of laying before you a representation of the condition and experience of Missouri during the progress of this rebellion, believing this only necessary to convince Your Excellency that the act of General McNeil in the premises was not only in accordance with the spirit of the general orders then and now in force in this department, but that it was the only measure which could restore peace and assure safety to the loyal citizens of Northern Missouri. In view of all the facts, therefore, your memorialists most heartily approve of the act of General McNeil as specified, and do hereby earnestly entreat the Government of the United States not to surrender that officer to those demanding him, but to approve and sustain his act in the premises, believing that in so doing he not only had in view and subserved the high and sacred interests of our whole country, but also showed himself to be a good soldier and a true and humane patriot.

Expressing the highest confidence in your administration, and the sincerest wish that the blessings of Heaven may attend your efforts to restore our country to a condition of perfect unity, peace, and prosperity, and assuring you that all our influence is given you in your endeavors to achieve such a glorious consummation, we remain your loyal fellow-citizens.*

*Numerously signed by citizens of Clarke, Lewis, and Shelby Counties.

"General Orders, no. 49." Halleck revised Lieber's draft portions on paroling and issued them separately from the subsequent "General Orders, no. 100." [WR, ser. II, vol. V, 306–7], 28 February, 1863.

GENERAL ORDERS, No. 49. — WAR DEPT., ADJT. GENERAL'S OFFICE, *Washington, February 28, 1863.*

I. The following rules in regard to paroles established by the common law and usages of war are published for the information of all concerned:

1. Paroling must always take place by the exchange of signed duplicates of a written document in which the name and rank of the parties paroled are correctly stated. Any one who intentionally misstates his rank forfeits the benefit of his parole and is liable to punishment.

2. None but commissioned officers can give the parole for themselves or their commands, and no inferior officer can give a parole without the authority of his superior if within reach.

3. No paroling on the battle-field. No paroling of entire bodies of troops after a battle and no dismissal of large numbers of prisoners with a general declaration that they are paroled is permitted or of any value.

4. An officer who gives a parole for himself or his command on the battle-field is deemed a deserter and will be punished accordingly.

5. For the officer the pledging of his parole is an individual act, and no wholesale paroling by an officer for a number of inferiors in rank is permitted or valid.

6. No non-commissioned officer or private can give his parole except through an officer. Individual paroles not given through an officer are not only void but subject the individuals giving them to the punishment of death as deserters. The only admissible exception is where individuals properly separated from their commands have suffered long confinement without the possibility of being paroled through an officer.

7. No prisoner of war can be forced by the hostile Government to pledge his parole, and any threat or ill-treatment to force the giving of the parole is contrary to the law of war.

8. No prisoner of war can enter into engagements inconsistent with his character and duties as a citizen and a subject of his State. He can only bind himself not to bear arms against his captor for a limited period, or until he is exchanged, and this only with the stipulated or implied consent of his Government. If the engagement which he makes is not approved by his Government he is bound to return and surrender himself as a prisoner of war. His own Government cannot at the same time disown his engagement and refuse his return as a prisoner.

9. No one can pledge his parole that he will never bear arms against the Government of his captors, nor that he will not bear arms against any other enemy of his Government not at the time the ally of his captors. Such agreements have reference only to the existing enemy and his existing allies and to the existing war and not to future belligerents.

10. While the pledging of the military parole is a voluntary act of the individual the capturing power is not obliged to grant it, nor is the Government of the individual paroled bound to approve or ratify it.

11. Paroles not authorized by the common law of war are not valid until approved by the Government of the individual so pledging his parole.

12. The pledging of any unauthorized military parole is a military offense punishable under the common law of war.

II. This order will be published at the head of every regiment in the service of the United States and will be officially communicated by every general commanding an army in the field to the commanding general of the opposing forces and will be hereafter strictly observed and enforced in the armies of the United States.*

By order of Maj. Gen. H. W. Halleck:

L. THOMAS,
Adjutant-General.

*This order was printed in circular form by General J. E. Johnston, through his assistant adjutant-general, Benjamin S. Ewell, and "published for the information of General Johnston's command."

Official orders dealing with the application of Lieber's essay on guerrilla warfare. [WR, ser. I, vol. XXII, part II, 237–44], 22 April, 1863.

GENERAL ORDERS, No. 30. — HDQRS. DEPT. OF THE MISSOURI, *Saint Louis, Mo., April 22, 1863.*

To warn the public of the severe penalties which will follow new transgressions in this department, and for the convenience of district commanders, judge-advocates, and military courts, the following laws of war and general instructions are prescribed. Judge-advocates will be governed accordingly in drawing their charges, and military courts in their findings, throughout this department:

I. THE SPY.—Some questions having arisen where authorities cannot be conveniently referred to as to what constitutes a spy, attention is invited to the following:

> Spies are persons who, in disguise, or under false pretenses, insinuate themselves among the enemy, in order to discover the state of his affairs, to pry into his designs, and then communicate to their employer the information thus obtained. . . . The term spy is frequently applied to persons sent to reconnoiter an enemy's position, his forces, defenses, &c., but not in disguise, or under false pretenses. Such, however, are not spies in the sense in which that term is used in military and international law; nor are persons so employed liable to any more rigorous treatment than ordinary prisoners of war. It is the disguise or false pretense which constitutes the perfidy and forms the essential elements of the crime, which, by the laws of war, is punishable with an ignominious death. (Halleck, International Law, chap. 16, sec. 26.)
>
> It may be added here that a person proved to be a regular soldier of the enemy's army, found in citizen's dress (disguise), within the lines of the captor, is universally dealt with as a spy. (Lieber.)
>
> If he (in the service of the enemy) comes in disguise or under false pretenses, for the purpose of obtaining military information,

he is a spy. If in the service of the enemy, and he comes in disguise, the law presumes him to be a spy. (Letter of instructions from Major-General Halleck, General-in-Chief.)

II. CORRESPONDENCE WITH THE ENEMY, MAIL CARRYING, &c.:

A person dwelling in a district under military occupation and giving information to the enemy is universally treated as a spy—a spy of a peculiarly dangerous character. . . . Even mere secret correspondence of a person in an occupied district, with the enemy, though the contents of the correspondence may have been innocent, has subjected the correspondent to serious consequences, and sometimes to the rigor of martial law, especially if the offense be committed after a proclamation to the contrary. . . . The spy becomes in this case peculiarly dangerous, making hostile use of the protection which, by the modern law of war, the victor extends to the persons and property of the conquered.

By the Fifty-seventh Article of War, whosoever shall be convicted of holding correspondence with, or giving intelligence to, the enemy, either directly or indirectly, shall suffer death, or such other punishment as shall be ordered by the sentence of a court-martial.

Persons engaged in carrying such correspondence will be held liable to the same punishment as the correspondents themselves.

III. GUERRILLA.—Under the general term of guerrilla will be more particularly considered:

1st. *Military Insurgents or War Rebels.*—The war rebel is defined by Lieber as follows:

Similar remarks [referring to those given under the preceding (sic) head] apply to the rebel, taking the word in the primitive meaning of *rebellare,* that is, to return to war after having been conquered, and to conspiracies, that is, secret agreements leading to such reassumption of arms in bands of whatever number, or which is still worse, plans to murder from secret places.

The war rebel has been universally treated with the utmost rigor of the military law. He exposes the occupying army to the greatest danger, and essentially interferes with the mitigation of the severity of war, which it is one of the noblest objects of the modern law of war to obtain. Whether the war rebel rises on his own account, or whether he has been secretly called upon by the enemy to do so, would make no difference whatever.

And particular attention is further called to the following extract from a letter of instructions, addressed by the General-in-Chief to the commanding general of this department:

> All of Missouri is now in the military occupation of the United States. The inhabitants are, therefore, bound by the laws of war (without any regard to their civil allegiance to the Government of the United States, as the sovereign power) to render obedience to the occupying military authority. If they take up arms in insurrection, or render aid and assistance to the enemy, they become military insurgents or military traitors, and thereby forfeit their lives and property. Every one who was not in arms at the time of the occupation, and who has not continued in arms, but who subsequently takes up arms within the territory militarily occupied by us, is not to be regarded as a prisoner of war, but is to be punished as a military insurgent. So everyone, be he a citizen of Missouri or not, who comes within our lines as a non-combatant, and afterward takes up arms, is a military insurgent.

The above remarks are applicable to all other parts of this department now in the military occupation of the United States.

Officers or men sent by the enemy within our lines to recruit, thereby inciting insurrection, become themselves (when not indeed actual spies) military insurgents. Such also are Knights of the Golden Circle, and members of other secret organizations looking to any opposition to the laws of the United States, being in the nature of conspirators.

Whoever shall be convicted as a military insurgent shall suffer death, according to the usages of nations, by sentence of a military commission.

2d. *The Partisan:*

> The partisan corps designates bodies detached from the main army. . . . The partisan leader commands a corps whose object is to injure the enemy by action separate from that of his own main army. The partisan acts chiefly upon the enemy's lines of connection and communication, and outside of or beyond the lines

> of operation of his own army, in the rear and on the flanks of the enemy. Rapid and varying movements and surprises are the chief means of his success; but he is part and parcel of the army, and, as such, considered entitled to the privileges of the laws of war, so long as he does not transgress them.

Partisan soldiers must have the organization and equipment of soldiers, or they are brigands or guerrillas, and will be punished as such.

3d. *The Brigand:*

> The brigand is, in military language, the soldier who detaches himself from his troop and commits robbery, naturally accompanied in many cases with murder and other crimes of violence. His punishment, inflicted even by his own authorities, is death. The word brigand, derived as it is from *briguer,* to beg, meant originally beggar, but it soon came to be applied to armed strollers, a class of men which swarmed in all countries in the middle ages. The term has, however, received a wider meaning in modern military terminology. He that assails the enemy without or against the authority of his own Government is called, even though his object should be wholly free from any intention of pillage, a brigand, subject to the infliction of death, if captured. . . . When Major Von Schill, commanding a Prussian regiment of huzzars, marched, in the year 1809, against the French, without the order of his Government, for the purpose of causing a rising of the people in the north of Germany, while Napoleon was occupied in the south with Austria, Schill was declared by Napoleon and his brother, a brigand; and the King of Westphalia, Jerome Bonaparte, offered a reward of 10,000 francs for his head. Schill was killed in battle; but 12 young officers of his troop, taken prisoners, were carried by the French to the Fortress Wesel, where a court-martial declared them prisoners of war. Napoleon quashed the finding, ordered a new court-martial, and they were all shot as brigands. Napoleon is not cited here as an authority in the law of war; he and many of his generals frequently substituted the harshest violence for martial usages. The case is mentioned as an illustration of the meaning attached to the word brigand in the law of war, and of the fact that death is the acknowledged punishment for the brigand.

Whoever shall be convicted as a brigand, no matter whether of our own forces or those of the enemy, shall suffer death, according to the usage of nations, by sentence of a military commission.

4th. *The Guerrilla Proper.*—Guerrillas proper may be defined as—

> Troops not belonging to a regular army, consisting of volunteers, perhaps self-constituted, but generally raised [within the lines of the enemy as a contradistinction from military insurgents] by individuals authorized to do so by the authority they acknowledge as their Government. They do not stand on the regular pay-roll of the army, or are not paid at all, take up arms and lay them down at intervals, and carry on petty war chiefly by raids, extortion, destruction, and massacre, and who cannot encumber themselves with many prisoners, and will, therefore, generally give no quarter. They are peculiarly dangerous, because they easily evade pursuit, and, by laying down their arms, become insidious enemies, because they cannot otherwise subsist than by rapine, and almost always degenerate into simple robbers or brigands.

Whoever shall be convicted as a guerrilla under this order shall suffer death, according to the usage of nations, by sentence of a military commission.

IV. RELIEVING THE ENEMY.—Fifty-sixth Article of War:

> Whoever shall relieve the enemy with money, victuals, or ammunition, or shall knowingly harbor or protect an enemy, shall suffer death, or such other punishment as shall be ordered by the sentence of a court-martial.

Those harboring and feeding guerrillas are included in this class, and will be so punished.

V. DISLOYAL PERSONS.—All persons not in the military service, who shall be convicted of disloyal expressions, oral, written, or printed, favoring the rebellion, shall be punished therefor by fine [assessment] or imprisonment, or both, or by being sent beyond the lines, by sentence of a military commission.

VI. TRANSGRESSION OF THE LAWS OF WAR is generally punishable by sentence of a military commission, and commanders will see that the strictest punishment is inflicted not less rigorously on the enemy than upon those of our own men who transgress them. It is only by strict adherence to these laws (and the more strict conformity should now be required because of the character of this war) that we can hope to restore peace to our distracted homes. We are at war with those who were brothers, friends, neighbors. They are now enemies. While we show them the severity of military power, we must not forget that it is our object to bring them back again to the relations enjoyed in past times, and all inflictions are only designed to subdue the rebellion.

Although assessments have been suspended in this department, they are not abrogated. No law of Congress or restraining order revokes the laws of war, which apply to confiscation of property to weaken the foe and strengthen ourselves. Property can and will be confiscated as occasion may justify. General Orders, No. 12, current series, of this department, relating to this matter, will be observed.

The following extracts from International Law, and Laws of War, by H. W. Halleck, now General-in-Chief of the Army, will suffice for field instructions:

CHAP. XIX.

• • • • •

SEC. 12. Private property on land is now, as a general rule of war, exempt from seizure or confiscation; and this general exemption extends even to cases of absolute and unqualified conquest. Some modern text writers—Hautefeuille, for example—contend for the ancient rule, that private property on land is subject to seizure and confiscation. They are undoubtedly correct with respect to the general abstract right, as deduced from the law of nature and ancient practice; but while the general right continues, modern usage and the opinions of modern text writers of the highest authority have limited this right by establishing the rule of general exemption. . . .

SEC. 13. But it must also be remembered that there are many exceptions to this rule, or rather that the rule itself is not by any means absolute or universal. The general theory of war is, as heretofore stated, that all private property may be taken by the conqueror, and such was the ancient practice. But the modern usage is not to touch private property on land, without making compensation, except in certain specified cases. These exceptions may be stated: . . . First. Confiscations or seizures by way of penalty for military offenses. Second. Forced contributions for the support of the invading armies, or as an indemnity for the expenses of maintaining order and affording protection to the conquered inhabitants. . . .

SEC. 14. In the first place, we may seize upon private property by way of penalty for the illegal acts of individuals, or of the community to which they belong. Thus, if an individual be guilty of conduct in violation of the laws of war, we may seize and confiscate the private property of the offender. So, also, if the offense attach itself to a particular community or town, all the individuals of that community or town are liable to punishment, and we may either seize upon their property or levy upon them a retaliatory contribution, by way of penalty. Where, however, we can discover and secure the individuals so offending, it is more just to inflict the punishment upon them only; but it is a general law of war that communities are accountable for the acts of their individual members. This makes it the interest of all to discover the guilty persons, and to deliver them up to justice. But if these individuals are not given up, or cannot be discovered, it is usual to impose a contribution upon the civil authorities of the place where the offense is committed, and these authorities raise the amount of the contribution by a tax levied upon their constituents. . . .

SEC. 15. In the second place, we have a right to make the enemy's country contribute to the expenses of the war. Troops, in the enemy's country, may be subsisted either by regular magazines, by forced requisitions, or by authorized pillage. It is not always politic, or even possible, to provide regular magazines for the entire supplies of an army during the active operations of a campaign. Where this cannot be done, the general is obliged either to resort to military requisitions or to intrust their subsistence to the troops themselves. The inevitable consequences of the latter system are universal pillage, and a total relaxation of discipline; the loss of private property, and the violation of individual rights, are usually followed by the massacre of straggling parties, and the ordinary peaceful and non-combatant inhabitants are converted into bitter and implacable enemies. The system is, therefore, regarded as both impolitic and unjust, and is coming into general disuse among the most civilized nations, at least for the support of the main army. In case of small detachments, where great rapidity of motion is requisite, it sometimes becomes necessary for the troops to procure their subsistence wherever they can. In such a case, the seizure of private property becomes a necessary consequence of the military operations, and is, therefore, unavoidable. Other cases of similar character might be mentioned. But even in most of these special and extreme cases provision might be made for subsequently compensating the owners for the loss of property.

SEC. 16. In the invasion of the Spanish peninsula, Napoleon had to choose between methodical operations, with provisions carried in the train of his army, or purchased of the inhabitants and regularly paid for, and irregular warfare, supplying his troops by forced requisitions and pillage. The former was adopted for some of the main armies, moving on prescribed lines, and the latter for the more active masses. Soult and Suchet, in favorable parts of the country, succeeded for a considerable length of time in procuring regular supplies for their armies, but most of the French generals obtained subsistence for their troops mainly by pillage. . . .

SEC. 17. Upon the invasion of Mexico by the armies of the United States, in 1846, the commanding generals were, at first, instructed to abstain from appropriating private property to the public use without purchase, at a fair price; but subsequently instructions of a severer character were issued. It was said by the American Secretary of War (Mr. Marcy) that an invading army had the unquestionable right to draw its supplies from the enemy without paying for them, and to require contributions for its support, and to make the enemy feel the weight of the war. He further observed that, upon the liberal principles of civilized warfare, either of three modes might be pursued to obtain supplies from the enemy: First, to purchase them in open market at such prices as the inhabitants of the country might choose to exact; second, to pay the owners a fair price, without regard to what they themselves might demand, on account of the enhanced value resulting from the presence of a foreign army; and, third, to require them as contributions, without paying or engaging to pay therefor.

• • • • • •

SEC. 22. While there is some uncertainty as to the exact limit fixed by the voluntary law of nations to our right to appropriate to our own use the property of an enemy, or to subject it to military contributions, there is no doubt whatever respecting its waste and useless destruction. This is forbidden alike by the law of nations and the rules of war. But if such destruction is necessary, in order to cripple the operations of the enemy, or to insure our own success, it is justifiable. Thus, if we cannot bring off a captured vessel, we may sink or burn it in order to prevent its falling into the enemy's hands; but we cannot do this in mere wantonness. We may destroy provisions and forage, in order to cut off the enemy's subsistence; but we cannot destroy vines and cut down fruit trees, without being looked upon as savage barbarians. We may demolish fortresses, ramparts, and all structures solely devoted to the purposes of war; but, as already stated, we cannot destroy public or private edifices of a civil character, temples of religion, and monuments of art, unless their destruction should become necessary in the operations of a siege, or in order to prevent their affording a lodgment or protection to the enemy.

VII. THE FOLLOWING LAWS passed by the last Congress are published for the information of all concerned:

AN ACT to prevent and punish frauds upon the Government of the United States. Approved March 2, 1863.

Be it enacted by the Senate and House of Representatives of the United States of America in Congress assembled, That any person in the land or naval forces of the United States, or in the militia in actual service of the United States, in time of war, who shall make or cause to be made, or present or cause to be presented for payment or approval to or by any person or officer in the civil or military service of the United States, any claim upon or against the Government of the United States, or any department or officer thereof, knowing such claim to be false, fictitious, or fraudulent; any person in such forces or service who shall, for the purpose of obtaining, or aiding in obtaining, the approval or payment of such claim, make, use, or cause to be made or used any false bill, receipt, voucher, entry, roll, account, claim, statement, certificate, affidavit, or deposition, knowing the same to contain any false or fraudulent statement or entry; any person in said forces or service who shall make or procure to be made, or knowingly advise the making of any false oath to any fact, statement, or certificate, voucher or entry, for the purpose of obtaining, or of aiding to obtain, any approval or payment of any claim against the United States or any department or officer thereof; any person in said forces or service who, for the purpose of obtaining or enabling any other person to obtain from the Government of the United States, or any department or officer thereof, any payment or allowance, or the approval or signature of any person in the military, naval, or civil service of the United States, of or to any false, fraudulent, or fictitious claim, shall forge or counterfeit, or cause or procure to be forged or counterfeited, any signature upon any bill, receipt, voucher, account, claim, roll, statement, affidavit, or deposition; and any person in said forces or service who shall utter or use the same as true or genuine, knowing the same to have been forged or counterfeited; any person in said forces or service who shall enter into any agreement, combination, or conspiracy to cheat or defraud the Government of the United States, or any department or officer thereof, by obtaining, or aiding and assisting to obtain, the payment or allowance of any false or fraudulent claim; any person in said forces or service who shall steal, embezzle, or knowingly and willfully misappropriate or apply to his own use or benefit, or who shall wrongfully and knowingly sell, convey, or dispose of any ordnance, arms, ammunition, clothing, subsistence stores, money, or other property of the United States, furnished or to be used for the military or naval service of the United States; any contractor, agent, paymaster, quartermaster, or other person whatsoever in said forces or service having charge, possession, custody, or control of any money or other public property, used or to be used in the military or naval service of the United States, who shall, with intent to defraud the United States, or willfully to conceal such money or other property, deliver or cause to be delivered to any other person having authority to receive the same any amount of such money or other public property less than that for which he shall receive a certificate or receipt; any person in said forces or service who is or shall be authorized to make or deliver any certificate, voucher, or receipt, or other paper certifying the receipt of arms, ammunition, provisions, clothing, or other public property so used or to be used, who shall make or deliver the same to any person without having full knowledge of the truth of the facts stated therein, and with intent to cheat, defraud, or injure the United States; any person in said forces or service who shall knowingly purchase or receive, in pledge for any obligation or indebtedness, from any soldier, officer, or other person called into or employed in said forces or service, any arms, equipments, ammunition, clothes, or military store, or other public property, such soldier, officer, or other person not having the lawful right to pledge or sell the same, shall be deemed guilty of a criminal offense, and shall be subject to the rules and regulations made for the government of the military and naval forces of the United States, and the militia when called into and employed in the actual service of the United States in time of war, and to the provisions of this act. And every person so offending may be arrested and held for trial by a court-martial, and if found guilty shall be punished by fine and imprisonment, or such other punishment as the court-martial may adjudge, save the punishment of death.

SEC. 2. *And be it further enacted,* That any person heretofore called or hereafter to be called into or employed in such forces or service, who shall commit any violation of this act and shall afterwards receive his discharge, or be dismissed from the service, shall, notwithstanding such discharge or dismissal, continue to be liable to be arrested and held for trial and sentence by a court-martial, in the same manner and to the same extent as if he had not received such discharge or been dismissed.

• • • • • •

AN ACT for enrolling and calling out the national forces, and for other purposes. Approved March 3, 1863.

• • • • • •

SEC. 21. *And be it further enacted,* That so much of the fifth section of the act approved seventeenth July, eighteen Hundred and sixty-two, entitled, "An act to amend an act calling forth the militia to execute the laws of the Union," and so forth, as requires the approval of the President to carry into execution the sentence of a court-martial, be, and the same is hereby, repealed, as far as relates to carrying into execution the sentence of any court-martial against any person convicted as a spy or deserter, or of mutiny or murder; and hereafter sentences in punishment of these offenses may be carried into execution upon the approval of the commanding general in the field.

SEC. 22. *And be it further enacted,* That courts-martial shall have power to sentence officers who shall absent themselves from their commands without leave, to be reduced to the ranks to serve three years or during the war.

SEC. 23. *And be it further enacted,* That the clothes, arms, military outfits, and accouterments furnished by the United States to any soldier, shall not be sold, bartered, exchanged, pledged, loaned, or given away; and no person not a soldier, or duly authorized officer of the United States, who has possession of any such clothes, arms, military outfits, or accouterments, furnished as aforesaid, and which have been the subjects of any such sale, barter, exchange, pledge, loan, or gift, shall have any right, title, or interest therein; but the same may be seized and taken wherever found by any officer of the United States, civil or military, and shall thereupon be delivered to any quartermaster, or other officer authorized to receive the same; and the possession of any such clothes, arms, military outfits, or accouterments, by any person not a soldier or officer of the United States, shall be *prima facie* evidence of such a sale, barter, exchange, pledge, loan, or gift, as aforesaid.

• • • • • •

SEC. 25. *And be it further enacted,* That every judge-advocate of a court-martial or court of inquiry hereafter to be constituted, shall have power to issue the like process to compel witnesses to appear and testify which courts of criminal jurisdiction within the State, Territory, or district where such military courts shall be ordered to sit may lawfully issue.

• • • • • •

SEC. 27. *And be it further enacted,* That depositions of witnesses residing beyond the limits of the State, Territory, or district in which military courts shall be ordered to sit, may be taken in cases not capital by either party, and read in evidence; provided the same shall be taken upon reasonable notice to the opposite party, and duly authenticated.

SEC. 28. *And be it further enacted,* That the judge-advocate shall have power to appoint a reporter, whose duty it shall be to record the proceedings of and testimony taken before military courts instead of the judge-advocate; and such reporter may take down such proceedings and testimony in the first instance in shorthand. The reporter shall be sworn or affirmed faithfully to perform his duty before entering upon it.

SEC. 29. *And be it further enacted,* That in time of war, insurrection, or rebellion, murder, assault and battery with an intent to kill, manslaughter, mayhem, wounding by shooting or stabbing with an intent to commit murder, robbery, arson, burglary, rape, assault and battery with an intent to commit rape, and larceny, shall be punishable by the sentence of a general court-martial or military commission, when committed by persons who are in the military service of the United States, and subject to the articles of war; and the punishments for such offenses shall never be less than those inflicted by the laws of the State, Territory, or district in which they may have been committed.

• • • • • •

SEC. 38. *And be it further enacted,* That all persons who, in time of war or of rebellion against the supreme authority of the United States, shall be found lurking or acting as spies, in or about any of the fortifications, posts, quarters, or encampments of any of the armies of the United States, or elsewhere, shall be triable by a general court-martial or military commission, and shall, upon conviction, suffer death.

VIII. The laws of war apply equally to all portions of our country while war exists, and they will be obeyed in all parts of this department. To secure prompt trial and punishment, district and corps commanders will have courts and commissions always ready to act summarily when occasion requires prompt punishment. Courts and commissions may be designated to accompany detached expeditions; the persons composing such courts not to be excused from field duty, except when actually trying a cause. When it is expedient, criminals will be turned over to the civil tribunals; but civil tribunals must not be used to embarrass or prevent military operations. When officers or soldiers transgress, they should be reported to superiors, who are required to redress wrongs inflicted on loyal and peaceable citizens, by turning the transgressor over to civil or military authority.

IX. Where an oath of allegiance is to be administered by the military authority, the following, and no other form, will be adopted:

> I solemnly swear that I will bear true allegiance to the United States, and support and sustain the Constitution and laws thereof; that I will maintain the national sovereignty paramount to that of all State, county, or Confederate powers; that I will discourage, discountenance, and forever oppose secession, rebellion, and the disintegration of the Federal Union; that I disclaim and denounce all faith and fellowship with the so-called Confederate armies, and pledge my honor, my property, and my life to the sacred performance of this my solemn oath of allegiance to the Government of the United States of America.
>
> Subscribed and sworn to before me this ________ day of ________, 1863.
>
> DESCRIPTION.
>
> Age, ________; height, ________; color of eyes, ________; color of hair, ________; characteristics, ________.

When a bond is required the following form is prescribed:

> Know all men by these presents, that we, ________, of ________, in the county of ________, and State of ________, as principal, and ________, as sureties, are held and firmly bound unto the United States of America, in the sum of ________ dollars, for the payment of which, well and truly to be made, we hereby bind ourselves, our heirs and assigns, firmly, by these presents. Sealed with our seals, and dated this ________ day of ________, A.D. 1863.
>
> The condition of the above obligation is such that whereas the above bounden ________ has been arrested on the charge of ________, and has been discharged from imprisonment upon his ________ and this bond.
>
> Now, if the said ________ shall carefully and truly observe all the terms and conditions of said ________, abstain from all words

or deeds tending to aid, encourage, or promote the existing rebellion against the authority of the United States, or to disturb the existing Government of the State of Missouri; and shall not, directly or indirectly, furnish information, arms, money, provisions, or any other commodity whatever to, or hold communication with, any person or persons engaged in hostilities against the Government of the United States or the State of Missouri, then this obligation is to be void. It is else to be in full force. And it is hereby understood and agreed that in case said ________ shall be found guilty of violating the conditions of this obligation or said ________ by any military commission or tribunal, appointed under orders of the commanding general to try such offenses, then any officer in the military service acting under orders from the department headquarters may seize and sell, or otherwise dispose of, any property of the above-named obligors, to an amount sufficient to satisfy the amount above named.

________ ________[seal.]
________ ________[seal.]
________ ________[seal.]

Uniformity in these matters is enjoined.

X. All proceedings of military courts will, as soon as practicable after confirmation, or necessary action by the convening authority, be transmitted through intermediate commanders to the judge-advocate at these headquarters.

XI. All newspapers within this department will give one insertion of this order in their columns, and forward a copy, with reasonable bill, to the assistant adjutant-general, at these headquarters.

By command of Major-General Curtis:

H. Z. CURTIS,
Assistant Adjutant-General.

Announcement of "General Orders, no. 100" [WR, ser. III, vol. III, 148–64], 24 April, 1863. Though dated officially in April, the Code was not actually published until early May, 1863.

GENERAL ORDERS, No. 100. } WAR DEPT., ADJT. GENERAL'S OFFICE, *Washington, April 24, 1863.*

The following instructions for the government of armies of the United States in the field, prepared by Francis Lieber, LL.D., and revised by a board of officers of which Maj. Gen. E. A. Hitchcock is president, having been approved by the President of the United States, he commands that they be published for the information of all concerned.

By order of the Secretary of War:

E. D. TOWNSEND,
Assistant Adjutant-General

The following exchange of correspondence is representative of attempts to apply the "General Orders, no. 100," particularly on the questions of "parole" and prisoner exchange.

Commanding General N. B. Buford, Cairo, Illinois, to Secretary of War E. M. Stanton, Washington. [WR, ser. II, vol. V, 521–2], 25 April, 1863.

Hon. E. M. STANTON, *Secretary of War.*

SIR: Your letter of the 21st instant is received. The instructions in it in reference to colored persons "captives of war" have and shall be faithfully carried out. It is not true that I have failed to afford them all the protection of my power "upon the ground that I have no sympathy with abolitionist" or any other ground. Personally I feel a deep sympathy with the colored refugees of the South who have escaped from slavery. I have published under my signature articles 15, 22, 23, and 33 of the code, received by me from General Hitchcock and Doctor Lieber, in the Chicago Tribune which is read by all General Grant's forces, believing that article 33 was of vast importance. On taking command of this post General Tuttle took with him the adjutant-general and left very scanty records of the post. He left me no record of his being "authorized to make arrangements with humane and benevolent persons in the State of Illinois to give them (the negroes) employment for their support." But I have understood that to be the design of the Government and have acted on it. I have given every respectable applicant of a free State permission to take any of these people under my charge to his home on condition that he support them in sickness as well as in health and [with] fair compensation. I have refused to let them be taken to Kentucky or the ports of Missouri opposite to this place. . . .

I am sorry to trouble you with so long a letter, but it seemed necessary that I should enter into details.

I have the honor to be, your obedient servant,

N. B. BUFORD,
Brigadier-General, Commanding.

Lieber, New York, to Halleck, Washington, 20 May, 1863. [HL]. The Knights of the Golden Circle, referred to below, were an incipient pro-Confederate body, in the southern areas of the Midwest that had been settled chiefly by "Southrons." Quasi-secret in the mode of the various bodies of self-styled "Knights" in the post-Civil War South, its potentialities were feared but it was successfully repressed.

My dear General,

I have the copy of Gen. Orders No. 100, which you sent me. I have not yet received the hundred copies promised by the Adj. Genl. I owe you—and so does the country—some three or four very important additions; the Generals of the Board have added some valuable parts, but there have also a few things been omitted, which I regret. That is natural. As the order now stands, I think the No. 100 will do honor to our country. It will be adopted as a basis for similar works by the English, French and Germans. It is a contribution by the U.S. to the stock of common civilisation. I feel almost sad in closing this business. Let me hope it will not put a stop, at least not an entire stop to our correspondence. I feel the sentiments of sincere friendship for you. I regret that your name is not visibly connected with this code. *You* do not regret it because you are void of ambition, to a faulty degree, as it seems to me. I do not say to you, as Richelieu said to Louis XIII, *Votre majeste est d'une secheresse remarquable* [Your Majesty has a remarkable dryness]—far from it, but I do not know, nor do I recollect ever having known a man, and especially a soldier so free from ambition, which leads you even to abstaining from putting yourself right with the public, when it would be necessary for the public weal to do so.

Some opportunity will occur I have no doubt and hope, when I shall yet chisel your name on this marble tablet of the code.

I am sorry that the words concluding [paragraph] 101 slipped in: "So dangerous" and "so difficult" are not dignified expressions in a code. I avoid them even in letters. Whose are they? I have no doubt they merely slipt in.

I wish I could see the charges against Vallandigham. A very important paper might be written on the limit of free speech, especially in times disturbed by war. Is it lawful to call on fellow beings to commit a crime—to steal, to poison, to set fire to a house? And wherever Government omits doing what is absolutely necessary there will be lynch law, courts, etc. The whole course of Vallandigham proves to my mind that he is a positive conspirator—a member of the Golden Circle. But what did he say, what did he do in that particular case?

Will you issue an order under your name, directing particular attention and obedience to No. 100?

I believe it is now time for you to issue a strong order, directing attention to those paragraphs in the Code which prohibit devastations, demolition of private property, etc. I know by letters from the West and the South, written by men on our side, of course, that the wanton destruction of property by our men is alarming. It does incalculable injury. It demoralizes our troops, it annihilates wealth irrevocably and makes a return to a state of peace and peaceful minds more and more difficult. Your order, though impressive and even sharp, might be written, with reference to the Code, and pointing out the disastrous consequences of reckless devastation, in a manner that it might not furnish our reckless enemy with new arguments for his savagery.

The accompanying, I have written separately, so that you might show it to the Secr. of War if you think necessary.

Did you observe that, in the line of order No. 100, my name is spelt Leiber instead of Lieber?

Ever your sincere friend,

Francis Lieber.

William H. Ludlow, Union Army Agent for Exchange of Prisoners, Fort Monroe, Virginia, to Robert Ould, Confederate Agent for Exchange of Prisoners, Richmond, Virginia. [WR, ser. II, vol. V, 690], 22 May, 1863.

Hon. ROBERT OULD, *Agent for Exchange of Prisoners.*

SIR: I have the honor to inclose to you copies of General Orders, No. 49 and No. 100, of War Department, announcing regulations and instructions for the government of the U.S. forces in the field in the matter of paroles. These together with the stipulations of the cartel will govern our army. I would invite your special attention to article 7 of the cartel which provides that all prisoners of war shall be sent to places of delivery therein specified. The execution of this article will obviate much discussion and difficulty growing out of the mode, time and place of giving paroles. No paroles or exchanges will be considered binding except those under the stipulations of said article and permitting commanders of two opposing armies to exchange or release on parole at other points mutually agreed on by said commanders.

I am, very respectfully, your obedient servant,

WM. H. LUDLOW,

Lieutenant-Colonel and Agent for Exchange of Prisoners.

Ludlow to Ould. [WR, ser. II, vol. V, 702] 25 May, 1863.

SIR: You threaten retaliation in your letter of the 22d instant in case certain parties whom you have demanded are not delivered to you. I beg leave to inform you that no deliveries of any kind will be made to you under such threats. If such threats are withdrawn deliveries can be made of parties properly entitled to release but not otherwise. Three-fourths or nine-tenths of the cases of which you have furnished memoranda have been released and delivered to you. If before the necessary investigations in the remaining cases have been made you put in practice retaliation either upon our officers or men I give you formal notice that the United States Government will exercise their discretion in selecting such persons as they think best, whether officers or privates, for the purpose of counter retaliation.

I am, very respectfully, your obedient servant,

Ould to Ludlow. [WR, ser. II, vol. V, 744] 5 June, 1863.

SIR: Will you be good enough to inform me when it is to be considered that General Orders, No. 100, went into effect. Is the date of the order April 24, 1863, or the date of its communication to me, 23d May, 1863, the true time? Do you recognize the rules of General Orders, No. 100, to be as binding against you as for you?

Permit me also to call your attention to the flagrant outrages that have recently been perpetrated in Gloucester, Mathews, King and Queen and the adjacent counties. Are they a fair interpretation of your celebrated general order? I am aware it gives a license for a man to be either a fiend or a gentleman. He can find abundant authority for either role in the order. What is the interpretation in General Dix's department? The country has always esteemed him as an honorable gentleman. I inclose a slip which is inside the truth recounting some of the doings of Colonel Kilpatrick. Does General Dix approve of his style of conducting war even with belligerent rebels? It is in his own department. Perhaps the higher powers may have something to do with this question some of these days. "Silent spectators of the destruction of their agricultural implements."

Respectfully, your obedient servant,

G. A. Schmitt, Captain, 20th Massachusetts Volunteers, to Henry Wilson, Congressman. [WR, ser. II, vol. V, 753] 6 June, 1863.

HEADQUARTERS SECOND DIVISION,
Convalescent Camp, June 6, 1863.

Hon. HENRY WILSON,
Member of Congress, Chairman Committee on Military Affairs.

HONORABLE SIR: I feel it my duty to draw your attention to a defect in the system of paroling prisoners of war. A number of such persons having lately come into camp I learned from officers and men the following facts:

1. That the rebels administer the oath to privates and non-commissioned officers direct and parole them in the absence of

officers of our Army. This is in direct violation of General Orders, No. 100, section VII, paragraph 126, issued April 24, 1863.

2. That the oath so administered contains the words "not to aid and abet the United States by bearing arms or otherwise" which is loose and too wide an application of parole, disquieting, by its contradiction to same order and section, paragraph 130, the consciences of the honest and affording a seemingly just excuse to the dishonest, who are opposed to military discipline after they come to Annapolis or here.

3. That the latest form of the oath concocted by the traitors contains a clause by which officers (I could not learn whether men also) are bound not to go into any camp or fortress or other place devoted to military purposes belonging to the United States until exchanged. This in direct conflict with orders establishing camps for paroled prisoners.

The officers and men from whom I learned these facts were taken prisoners between May 2 and 5 and sent to Annapolis May 14 from City Point. The order from our Government must have been communicated to the rebels before that time, having been issued April 24. The additional clause forbidding any military discipline seems to have been the answer to the liberal and just provisions of Orders, No. 100. The state of discipline and cleanliness at Annapolis or rather absence of either seems to be shocking if the statement of officers and gentlemen are to be believed. I know of an officer who went to New York from there and staid five days. All the officers describe it as the filthiest place they have seen. We can keep our camp clean. The soldiers (paroled) are not made to do anything there. When they came here we had very hard work to get them to obey orders. They were very unclean.

I have the honor to be, sir, very respectfully, your obedient servant,

G. A. SCHMITT,

Captain, Twentieth Mass. Vols., Comdg. Second Div. Convalescents.

Ludlow to W. Hoffman, Union Army [WR, ser. II, vol. V, 753 and 755–6] 6 and 7 June, 1863.

FORT MONROE, *June 6, 1863.*

Col. W. HOFFMAN, *Commissary-General of Prisoners:*

On the 22d May I gave to Mr. Ould General Orders, Nos. 49 and 100, with notice that no paroles would be binding after that date except those under the stipulation of article 7 of the cartel which provides for the delivery of prisoners at certain points unless otherwise agreed upon by commanders of opposing armies. Please send me copies of all orders of courts-martial in cases of execution.

WM. H. LUDLOW,
Lieutenant-Colonel, &c.

* * * * * *

June 7, 1863.

COLONEL: What information have you in relation to the effect of the time when General Orders, No. 100, went into effect? It was served upon Mr. Ould on the 23d of May last (as I telegraphed to you) with the notice that all captures must be reduced to possession as provided for in article 7 of the cartel. Am I correct in the supposition that Orders, No. 100 is to be recognized as binding against us as for us?

I am, very respectfully, your obedient servant,
WM. H. LUDLOW,

D. Hunter, Major-General, to James Montgomery, Colonel, stressing the protection of fugitives. [WR, ser. I, vol. XIV, 466–7] 9 June, 1863.

HEADQUARTERS DEPARTMENT OF THE SOUTH,
Hilton Head, S. C., June 9, 1863.

Col. JAMES MONTGOMERY,
Comdg. Second S. C. Regiment, Saint Simon's Island:

COLONEL: I have the honor of transmitting herewith a copy of General Orders, No. 100. of the War Department, current series, promulgating a system of "Instructions for the government of armies of the United States in the field," prepared by an eminent international and military jurist, Dr. Francis Lieber, revised by a board of high officers, and approved and established by the President of the United States.

To sections I, II, III of these instructions I beg to call your particular attention; not that in any manner I doubt the justice or generosity of your judgment, but for the reason that it is peculiarly important, in view of the questions which have heretofore surrounded the employment of colored troops in the armies of the United States, to give our enemies (foreign and domestic) as little ground as possible for alleging any violation of the laws and usages of civilized warfare as a palliation for these atrocities which are threatened against the men and officers of commands similar to your own. If, as is threatened by the rebel Congress, this war has eventually to degenerate into a barbarous and savage conflict, softened by none of the amenities and rights established by the wisdom and civilization of the world through successive centuries of struggle, it is of the first moment that the infamy of this deterioration should rest exclusively and without excuse upon the rebel Government. It will therefore be necessary for you to exercise the utmost strictness in insisting upon compliance with the instructions herewith sent, and you will avoid any devastation which does not strike immediately at the resources or material of the armed insurrection which we are now engaged in the task of suppressing.

All fugitives who come within our lines you will receive, welcome, and protect. Such of them as are able-bodied men you will at once enroll and arm as soldiers. You will take all horses and mules available for transportation to the enemy; also all cattle and other food which can be of service to our forces. As the rebel Government has laid all grain and produce under conscription, to be taken at will for the use of its armed adherents, you will be justified in destroying all stores of this kind which you shall not be able to remove; but the destruction of crops in the ground, which may not be fit for use until the rebellion is over, or which may when ripe be of service to the forces of our Government occupying the enemy's country, you will not engage in without mature consideration. This right of war, though unquestionable in certain extreme cases, is not to be lightly used, and if wantonly used might fall under that part of the instructions which prohibits devastation. All household furniture, libraries, churches, and hospitals you will of course spare.

That the wickedness and folly of the enemy may soon place us in a position where the immutable laws of self-defense and the stern necessity of retaliation will not only justify but enjoin every conceivable species of injury is only to be too clearly apprehended; but until such time shall have arrived, and until the proof, not merely of declarations of resolves but of acts, is unmistakable, it will be both right and wise to hold the troops under your command to the very strictest interpretation of the laws and usages of civilized warfare.

Expressing the highest confidence in your courage, skill, humanity, and discretion, I have the honor to be, colonel, very respectfully, yours,

D. HUNTER,
Major-General, Commanding.

Hoffman to Ludlow. [WR, ser. II, vol. V, 767] 9 June, 1863.

OFFICE COMMISSARY-GENERAL OF PRISONERS,
Washington, D.C., June 9, 1863.

Lieut. Col. W. H. LUDLOW,
Agent for Exchange of Prisoners, Fort Monroe, Va.

COLONEL: Your two letters of the 7th are received. I have forwarded to you at three different times orders which have been published, announcings of courts-martial in the cases of rebel spies and others sentenced to death, all of which I hope reached you safely. General Orders, No. 100, went into effect with us as soon as published. We hold the enemy bound by it from the time you presented it to Mr. Ould and it is as operative against us as for us. Its provisions so far as paroles are concerned are about the same as General Orders, No. 49, which I stated in my letter to you of the 20th ultimo was in force from the time it was published to the army, and all paroles taken or given in violation of it are not binding except in some particular cases when for special reasons generals commanding think proper to recognize paroles heretofore given by our troops. The enemy can take no exceptions to our recognizing irregular paroles which they have exacted. No such cases will occur hereafter. A few days since I returned to the Army of the Potomac a roll of prisoners of war captured and paroled by General Stoneman's command with the decision of the General-in-Chief that the paroles were not valid inasmuch as they had been taken in violation of General Orders, No. 49.

The State of Maine will leave tomorrow with some 300 prisoners of war and about forty citizen prisoners for delivery at City Point. Among them is Surg. W. A. McCorkle, Second Tennessee [Cavalry] Regiment, who under the cartel should be unconditionally released, but under present circumstances while they refuse to deliver the officers they hold you will decide on the propriety of holding or delivering him as may seem best to you.

I inclose to you a letter addressed to me by Surgeon Hewitt, of General Grant's army, in which he requests a statement made by Right Rev. Bishop Breen, of Jackson, Miss., in relation to the murder of Col. John N. Cromwell in the streets of Jackson, Miss., which he placed in the hands of General Winder, may be returned to him. The importance which attaches to this document will be apparent to you and will I am sure secure your immediate attention.

I send you by this mail some rolls of rebel prisoners of war paroled in the West some months since with certificate showing that they were delivered within the rebel lines. I am not sure you will be able to use them.

Very respectfully, your obedient servant,

W. HOFFMAN,

Ludlow to Ould. [WR, ser. II, vol. VI, 18] 14 June, 1863.

SIR: General Orders, No. 100, is considered as having gone into effect from the date of its communication to you on the 23d of May last, and is of course mutually binding.

I am, very respectfully, your obedient servant,

SIR: Doctor Green will be retained as a hostage for Doctor Rucker. All other surgeons in our custody (three or four now being here) will be released and delivered to you on the release and delivery to me of all you hold, except Doctor Rucker.

Do you agree to this, with the additional understanding that the detentions of surgeons shall be confined to these two?

Please inform me when Spencer Kellogg and other of our officers declared exchanged will be delivered at City Point, in order that arrangements may be made for sending up such of your exchanged officers as are at Fort Norfolk awaiting delivery.

I am, very respectfully, your obedient servant,

Hoffman to Hunter. [WR, ser. II, vol. VI, 21] 16 June, 1863.

OFFICE COMMISSARY-GENERAL OF PRISONERS,
Washington, D.C., June 16, 1863.

GENERAL: The following are extracts from a letter some days since addressed to Lieutenant-Colonel Ludlow, agent for exchange of prisoners, in relation to paroling of prisoners of war, to be laid before the Confederate commissioner as the rule which will govern the U.S. armies in the field:

> I inclose herewith General Orders, Nos. 49 and 100, current series, announcing regulations and instructions for the government of the U.S. forces in the field in the matter of paroles. These, together with the stipulations of the cartel, will govern our army. By the cartel all prisoners of war are to be delivered at certain named places, there to be exchanged or paroled, and all paroles exacted or accepted by the enemy from our troops in violation of its stipulations, except in the case provided for by the cartel, are null and void, and troops so paroled will be ordered to duty as if no parole had been given. Officers or soldiers who give paroles in violation of General Orders, No. 49, commit an offense for which they are liable to trial by a court-martial; but the enemy have, nevertheless, no right to claim that the parole is binding . . . Orders will be immediately issued from commanders to permit no paroles to be taken from the enemy except as provided for by the cartel, and all paroles now in force not so taken will be declared of no effect. Paroles given before the publication to the army of General Orders, No. 49, though deliveries were

not made as required by the cartel, will, under the usage prevailing at the time, be considered as valid.

There may be cases of a subsequent date where, from peculiar circumstances, it would be advisable to recognize irregular paroles, but in all such cases a special report, with full rolls of the parties, should be forwarded to this office as early as practicable.

Very respectfully, your obedient servant,

W. HOFFMAN,

Colonel Third Infantry and Commissary-General of Prisoners.

(Same to Maj. Gen. J. G. Foster, commanding Department of North Carolina, New Berne, N.C., and Maj. Gen. John E. Wool, commanding Department of the East, New York City, N.Y.)

Hoffman, Washington, to Gideon Welles, Union Secretary of Navy, Washington. [WR, ser. II, vol. VI, 23–4] 18 June, 1863.

Hon. GIDEON WELLES,

Secretary of the Navy, Washington, D.C.:

SIR: I have the honor to acknowledge the receipt of your letter of the 17th instant, accompanying a descriptive roll of 113 soldiers of the rebel army captured and paroled at the Yazoo hospital on the 21st May last.

I have the honor to inclose herewith General Order, No. 49 of the 28th February, and No. 100 of the 24th April, 1863, from the War Department, establishing rules for the government of the armies of the United States under which paroles are to be given or received, and I have also the honor to submit extracts from a letter which, by authority of the General-in-Chief, I addressed to Lieutenant-Colonel Ludlow, agent for the exchange of prisoners of war, instructing him how said orders are to be put in force. . . . I respectfully submit the matter for your consideration.

Very respectfully, your obedient servant,

W. HOFFMAN,

Colonel Third Infantry and Commissary-General of Prisoners.

Ould to Ludlow [WR, ser. II, vol. VI, 29] 19 June, 1863.

SIR: On the 5th day of June, 1863, I requested you to inform me when General Orders, No. 100, was to be considered as going into effect. To that you have returned no answer. Its date is April 24, 1863. You delivered it to me on the 23d of May, 1863.

I perceive by a General Order, No. 15, March 9 [8] , 1863, issued by General Schenck, that all officers and men who had been captured in his department, and particularly in the Shenandoah Valley, and released on parole, and not regularly exchanged should return to duty and service, on penalty of being considered deserters. When you delivered General Orders, No. 100, to me, I inquired of you as to the date when it went into effect. I understood you to say the date of its delivery. You may, therefore, well imagine my surprise when I perceive that, by the general order of one of your own departmental commanders, the new provisions as to paroles are not only to have effect from and after March 9, 1863, but are made to apply to all cases previous to that date, without any limitation as to time. This is not only contrary to your own declarations to me, but to our common practice up to May 23, 1863. You have charged against me and received credit for several captures made by General Stoneman's command in his recent raid. Is it pretended that you are to have credit for captures made by your commands, while none is to be given to us, under precisely the same circumstances? Is this fair, or just, or right?

Respectfully, your obedient servant,

Ludlow to Hoffman, [WR, ser. II, vol. VI, 33] 22 June, 1863.

COLONEL: I inclose to you a letter left with me by the officer in charge of Daniel Dusky. Can you furnish me other evidence that Jacob Varner is not now in their lines? Please do so if possible. General Orders, No. 100, was served upon Mr. Ould on the 23d of May last, and takes effect after that date. The service was accompanied with the notice, a copy of which I have before given you, that all captures must be reduced to possession and delivered at certain points agreed upon. If you have any paroles taken before that date, please send them and I can use them. The General

Orders, No. 15, March 7 [8], 1863, of Major-General Schenck is null and void, and subjects the parties interested in it to harsh treatment in the case of capture. If they gave their parole in violation of orders they should be punished, not debarred exchange.

I am, very respectfully, your obedient servant,

James A. Seddon, Confederate Secretary of War, Richmond, to Ould, denouncing the "General Orders, no. 100." [WR, ser. II, vol. VI, 41–7] 24 June, 1863.

CONFEDERATE STATES OF AMERICA, WAR DEPARTMENT,
Richmond, Va., June 24, 1863.

Hon. ROBERT OULD, *Agent of Exchange:*

SIR: In considering the Order No. 100, of 1863, U.S. War Department, entitled, "Instructions for the government of armies in the field," the inquiry is suggested whether it was communicated to you with any purpose of obtaining a reply from you as to the merits of the order or your assent to its provisions. It sometimes happens with nations engaged in war that besides the usual agreements relative to the exchange of prisoners, flags of truce, passports, and intercourse between armies in the field, general conventions are made for regulating the principles on which the war is to be conducted; the treatment that persons and property found in the territory which is the seat of the war shall experience, and how the evils of the war may be mitigated by the adoption of a positive code.

The writers on international law mention such conventions as entirely legitimate; but his order seems to repudiate such a purpose by asserting that "no conventional restriction of the modes adopted to injure the enemy is any longer admitted." Order No. 100 is a confused, unassorted, and undiscriminating compilation from the opinion of the publicists of the last two centuries, some of which are obsolete, others repudiated; and a military commander under this code may pursue a line of conduct in accordance with principles of justice, faith, and honor, or he may justify conduct correspondent with the warfare of the barbarous hordes who overran the Roman Empire, or who, in the Middle Ages, devastated the continent of Asia and menaced the civilization of Europe. There is no course left us but to designate the class of principles that meet our approbation and to distinguish those that will provoke retaliation. The Confederate States agree "that it is incumbent upon all who are in situations to administer martial law that they should be strictly guided by the principles of justice, honor, and humanity—virtues adorning a soldier even more than other men, for the very reason that he possesses the power of his arms against the unarmed—and that the law of war disclaims all cruelty and bad faith concerning engagements concluded with the enemy during the war, all extortions, all transactions for individual gain, all acts of private revenge, or connivance at such acts." They agree "that as civilization has advanced so has likewise steadily advanced, especially in war on land, the distinction between the private individual belonging to a hostile country and the hostile country itself with its men in arms. The principle has been more and more acknowledged that the unarmed citizen is to be spared in person, property, and honor as much as the exigencies of war will admit." They agree "that it is a violation of the laws of war and the principles of humanity to murder, enslave, or carry off to distant parts private citizens, and that the inoffensive individual should be as little disturbed in his private relations as the commander of the hostile troops can afford to grant in the overruling exigencies of a vigorous war." They agree "that it was in remote times, and continues to be with vindictive, malignant, and savage armies at the present time, the rule that the private individual of the hostile country is destined to suffer every privation of liberty and protection and every disruption of family ties, and that in modern regular wars of the Europeans and" portions of "their descendants in other portions of the globe"—candor will not allow us to say all of their descendants—"protection of the inoffensive citizen of the hostile country is the rule, and privation and disturbance of private relations is the exception." They acknowledge "that when men take up arms against one another in a public war they do not cease on this account to be moral beings, responsible to one another and to God."

These principles condemn the murder of non-combatants; the pillage of the farms and houses of persons who are not engaged in the war; the destruction of implements of husbandry, growing crops, mills, houses, fruit trees, and the filling up and destruction of ports and harbors of refuge; the expulsion of old men, women, and children, with limited supplies of money and clothing from their homes; the violation of cartels relative to the exchange of prisoners; the detention of prisoners for weeks and months, and even years, after their exchanges, and the inciting of slaves to insurrection.

Had no other articles upon the mode of prosecuting the war than those been published by the Government of the United States, Order No. 100 would have been regarded as a solemn rebuke by the compilers of its code to those military authorities by whom and to whom it is addressed of their conduct and practices during this war. The assertion of dogmas of another class become, therefore, necessary to afford some sort of an apology for this conduct and these practices.

I proceed to state these, that the two contradictory and opposed systems of what are designated as instructions, and what are selected as established rules and usages of war, may be confronted. "Military necessity," says Order No. 100, "admits of all direct destruction of life and limb of armed enemies, and of other persons whose destruction is incidentally unavoidable in the armed contests of the war; it allows of the capturing of every armed enemy, and every enemy of importance to the hostile Government, or of peculiar danger to the captor; it allows of all destruction of property, and obstruction of the ways and channels of traffic, travel, or communication, and of all withholding of sustenance or means of life from the enemy; of appropriation of whatever an enemy's country affords for the subsistence and safety of the army, and of such deception as does not involve the breaking of good faith, positively pledged, regarding agreements entered into during the war, or supposed by the modern law of war to exist." "War is not carried on by arms alone. It is lawful to starve the hostile belligerents, armed or unarmed, so that it leads to the speedier subjection of the enemy."

"Commanders, whenever admissible, inform the enemy of their intention to bombard a place, so that non-combatants, and especially the women and children, may be removed before the bombardment commences; but it is in no infraction of the law of war to omit thus to inform the enemy. Surprise may be a necessity."

These selections from the code will sufficiently discriminate the two classes of doctrine and the opposing systems that our enemies have presented in the same instructions. The war that the United States is carrying on against the Confederate States is a war opposed to the fundamental principle of their own Constitution. The overthrow of the principle of self-government, as recognized in the Declaration of Independence, and as embodied in the State and Federal Constitution of the States composing the Federal Union, which existed until 1860, is the principle which lies at the foundation of the military operations of the Federal Government. The subjugation of the Confederate States is the illegitimate object they propose to accomplish by the war.

To accomplish it they have established a military despotism upon the ruins of the Constitution of the United States and have adopted a barbarous system of warfare on the pretext of a military necessity. It is in this code of military necessity that the acts of atrocity and violence which have been committed by the officers of the United States and have shocked the moral sense of civilized nations are to find an apology and defense.

The history of this war exhibits frequently the murder in cold blood of unarmed and unresisting citizens; the destruction of small towns and villages as a pastime; the removal to distant places of a large number of citizens who at no time have been engaged with the army; the spoliation of farm-houses of their food, furniture, libraries, pictures, and family apparel by soldiers and in some cases by officers highest in command in the department. Men, women, and children have been expelled from their homes in the inclement weather of winter or in the darkness of night. It is shockingly true that our enemy does not carry on war alone by arms. It is not true that any military necessity excuses systematic and habitual departure from the laws of war first enunciated and justifies the adoption of rules contrary to them to regulate military operations. Military necessity as a legislator has a supreme authority; but the range of its jurisdiction is limited. The necessity must be present, urgent, and overruling, and the acts done under it must afford probable means of escape from an impending danger.

In such a case ordinary rules are suspended and what is fairly and reasonably done is sanctioned. Even justice and right in such cases withdraw their censorship and sway and submit temporarily to this more imperious authority; but no country, no government, is justified in deducing a rule of practice from rare and extreme instances of inexorable or unreasoning necessity. The judgment and conscience are alike perplexed in forming conclusions when measures of violence under such prompting are prescribed for their consideration, and the historian and publicist content themselves with narrating the facts and suggesting the extenuating circumstances in such occurrences without venturing to afford them countenance or approval.

The rulers or commanders who use them as precedents and indicate to their subordinates that there is some law of military necessity which it is competent for them to adopt as an habitual standard of conduct become *particeps criminis* in the atrocities that may follow and are worthy of the same degree of infamy and punishment. They cannot frame mischief into a code or make an instituted system of rules embodying the spirit of mischief under the name of a military necessity. The country that adopts as allies murder, rapine, cruelty, incendiarism, and revenge is condemned by the voice of the civilized world.

The war that needs such auxiliaries carries infallible marks to distinguish it as an unholy and unchristian war.

The answer to these doctrines of military necessity is to be found in that title of the same code which relates to the subject of retaliation. It is not at all surprising that those who would make a law-giver of military necessity should desire the abduction or dethronement of the rule of military retaliation, and so in this code retaliation is deprecated. A malignant, unscrupulous, revengeful enemy "leaves to his opponent no other means of securing himself against the repetition of barbarous outrage than is afforded by retaliation." The Confederacy acknowledges the obligation to employ retaliation carefully and with circumspection. The infliction of merited punishment upon notorious offenders against law and humanity should always be characterized by a judicial moderation and temperance. It should not be employed as an instrument of cruelty or revenge, and should not be carried any further than to produce a thorough reformation of the offending nation.

To this extent the Confederate States have asserted their determination to resort to it. In the military orders of this Department, bearing date August 1, 1862, the military orders of General Pope, commanding the Army of the United States in Northern Virginia, were reviewed, and the mode and measure of redress, which practices of a similar nature would provoke, plainly declared.

Again, on December 24, 1862, the President of the Confederate States published his proclamation in reference to the military administration of Maj. Gen. B. F. Butler. These public and authoritative expositions by the Confederate States of the laws and usages of war may be referred to as indicative of their temper and disposition that any practice on these institutes concerning necessity will incite.

The authorities who have issued Order No. 100 affect to be governed in the prosecution of this war by laws not prescribed by themselves, nor the offspring of their interest or passions, but which are derived from the usages of civilized nations, and have the sanction of the judgments of enlightened publicists. Nor do they openly contest the claim of the Confederate States to the full benefit of those laws.

The employment of a servile insurrection as an instrument of war is contrary to the usages of civilized nations, and the United States, under the counsel that prevailed in the better days of the Republic, would have regarded an attempt of the kind as dishonoring to the State or people who might be guilty of adopting it.

Since the existence of American Independence every one of its States recognized negro slavery as a legal relation within its limits, and its commercial population participated in the profits of the

African slave-trade under the laws of the Union after the commencement of the present century. The ratio upon which representation in one of the branches of their Congress, and their direct taxes are apportioned, is settled with reference to the existence of a population of bondsmen within the limits of the Union.

The highest judicial tribunal has determined that slavery and the slave trade are not contrary to the law of nations, and that the voluntary removal of slaves to a State where slavery does not exist does not prevent the renewal of the relation of master and slave on their return to the State of their domicile.

The diplomatic correspondence, the solemn treaties of the United States, show reclamations for the value of escaping slaves and of slaves abducted by a military force in time of war, and the recognition of that claim by the foreign nation. At this moment the Constitution and laws of the United States contain provisions for the return of fugitive slaves from one State to another. The principle of *postliminium* does not rest upon any fiction, nor is it any exceptional rule existing in the international law. The municipal laws of one State have no more authority or recognition within the limits of another than it is consistent with the law or policy of the latter to permit.

In those States in which slavery is prohibited the claim of the foreign master for the services or the custody of his slave whom he has imported is not recognized or enforced during his sojourn, and the slave may appeal to the civil tribunals for protection in case the attempt to maintain it is made; but the law of the State of the temporary domicile or sojourn is not recognized or enforced in the State to which the master and slave belong and the claim of the master will be upheld on his return. This proposition is exceedingly clear, and the most eminent jurists of the United States and Great Britain have sanctioned it and the texts of the Roman Pandects are consonant to it: *"Si vero servus transfugerit ad hostes; quoniam et cum casu captus est, dominus in eo postliminium habet."* The articles of the code on this subject are a specimen of pedantic impertinence without a parallel. The enlistment of negro slaves as a part of the Army of the United States cannot be regarded as having any object but one. It is a part of the system of the United States Government to subvert by violence the social system and domestic relations of the negro slaves in the Confederacy and to add to the calamities of the war a servile insurrection. The savage passions and brutal appetites of a barbarous race are to be stimulated into fierce activity.

Such a war involves necessarily the abandonment of all rules, conventions, mitigating influences, and humanizing usages. The enemy who adopts such auxiliaries proclaims in advance his desire as well as design that the war shall be one for mutual extermination. The Congress of the Confederate States at their last session adopted resolutions which have the force of laws in the Confederate States. They are the only reply that the Department has to make to the articles of the code and the practice of the United States on this subject.

The articles of Military Order No. 100 upon the subject of the exchange or parole of prisoners require a passing notice. The persons to be considered as prisoners of war, those to be released as non-combatants, and the terms on which the former should be exchanged, may be regulated by cartels agreed upon by the belligerents, or in the absence of such agreements on the usages of war and the particular instructions given to the commander of the capturing force by his government. The law of nations authorize the dismissal of prisoners on their parole under promise not to carry arms for a certain time or during the continuance of the war. They affirm that a commander may make engagements with the enemy to this effect; but such engagements have their limits; the limits suggested are that he cannot undertake that his troops shall never bear arms again against the enemy, though he may engage that they shall not do so during the existing war, because the enemy may so long detain them in captivity. It is obviously proper that the possession of the prisoner should be complete, *jure victoriae,* by the conqueror and the *spes recuperandi* frustrated. Hence the paroling of prisoners on the battle field before the contest is ended is inoperative and void. But this Department does not consent to the claim of the United States to determine when or under what circumstances the parole of a prisoner may take place. They may punish their soldiers for giving a parole or accepting a release contrary to or in the absence of their regulations; but the contract of parole being recognized as one lawful between the captor and the prisoner by the law of war, the government of the prisoner is bound to respect a fair and reasonable contract under which the prisoner has been released.

In the Regulations of the Army of the United States, revised by General Scott in 1825, the following institutes on that subject will be found:

(Extract from General Regulations for the Army of the United States, revised by Major-General Scott, 1825. . . .)

Paragraph 715, page 141. The officers among the prisoners will not, in general, be confined with the other prisoners. The general-in-chief, or the commander of a department, may, according to instructions and the deportment of the officers, give them permission to repair, without escort, to such places and by such routes as may be designated, taking from each his parole in writing, binding him to act accordingly.

Paragraph 716, page 141. Every such officer who violates his parole, by departing from the route prescribed or the limits assigned him, or who, being permitted to return to his own country, shall serve against the United States or their allies, before exchanged, or in violation of his parole given, every such officer being retaken shall, at least, be put and kept in irons, and may be otherwise punished, according to the particular circumstances of the case, the instructions of the Government, and the usages of war.

N. B.—General Scott in Mexico, especially at Puebla, paroled large numbers of Mexican soldiers without cartel or concert with the enemy. . . . The fact is stated in the title of Military Order No. 100 that it was proposed by a German professor, an alien by nativity to the Constitution, laws, and institutions of the United States. The intrinsic evidence furnished by the order itself shows that it is the handicraft of one much more familiar with the decrees of the imperial despotisms of the continent of Europe than with Magna Charta, the Petition of Right, the Bill of Rights, the

Declaration of Independence, and the Constitution of the United States.

The words war-traitor, war-rebel, are not words of an American vocabulary. Treason is defined in the Constitution of the United States; the evidence by which it is to be proved is described, and the judicial tribunals for the arraignment and trial of the traitor are established and determined by that instrument in words so plain that he that runs may read. The Constitution of the Confederate States contains the same provisions. It is exceedingly clear that martial law and military commissions can have no jurisdiction over one from whom allegiance is claimed because he is a traitor to the obligations that relation imposes. Imperial or military despots on the continent of Europe have employed commissions composed of military subordinates to accomplish their State policy, or gratify their revenge, but the faithful historian has recorded the reproving judgment of mankind upon the injustice of the procedure.

The Confederate States will perform another duty to the cause of American liberty by resisting to a bloody issue the employment of any such methods by our enemies in the course of this war in respect to any citizen of the Confederate States, either within or without the lines of the enemy, as a war-rebel or war-traitor, as defined by this order.

The most prominent of the matters treated of in Order No. 100 have been noticed. There are other articles that are objectionable, and that disclose the unrelenting and vindictive spirit with which our enemies prosecute the odious purpose which they have proposed to themselves to accomplish. The accomplishment of that purpose would be the overthrow of their own institutions, as well as of our own. The events of the war have sufficiently shown that our object has been to bring it to a conclusion, without impairing or weakening the institutions or principles that have come to us from our ancestors. We have not prosecuted war as an instrument of massacre or confusion, but in the maintenance of rights which were achieved for us by the expenditure of blood and treasure, and for which our fathers endured suffering and privations.

We have always been ready to frame conventions to mitigate its calamities, and to render a speedy and permanent peace attainable. We shall not depart from this course unless fairly justified by the great law of self-preservation, produced by a fatal necessity, created by the odious measures of our adversary.

JAMES A. SEDDON,
Secretary of War.

William F. Barry, Brigadier-General, Washington, to G. W. Cullum, Brigadier-General. [WR, ser. I, vol. XI, 349–50] 25 August, 1863.

HDQRS. INSPECTOR OF ARTILLERY, U.S. ARMY,
Washington, August 25, 1863.

Brig. Gen. G. W. CULLUM,
Chief of Staff, Headquarters of the Army.

GENERAL: In reply to your note of to-day's date I have to state for the information of Dr. Lieber as follows:

When it was believed at daybreak May 4, 1862, that the enemy had evacuated Yorktown and its defenses, our pickets and skirmishers and subsequently larger bodies of our troops immediately advanced to occupy the abandoned lines. Before reaching the glacis of the main work, and at the distance of more than 100 yards from it, several of our men were injured by the explosion of what was ascertained to be loaded shells buried in the ground. These shells were the ordinary 8 or 10 inch mortar or columbiad shells, filled with powder, buried a few inches below the surface of the ground, and so arranged with some fulminate, or with the ordinary artillery friction primer, that they exploded by being trod upon or otherwise disturbed. In some cases articles of common use, and which would be most likely to be picked up, such as engineers' wheelbarrows, or pickaxes, or shovels, were laid upon the spot with apparent carelessness. Concealed strings or wires leading from the friction primer of the shell to the superincumbent articles were so arranged that the slightest disturbance would occasion the explosion. These shells were not thus placed on the glacis at the bottom of the ditch, &c., which, in view of an anticipated assault, might possibly be considered a legitimate use of them, but they were basely planted by an enemy who was secretly abandoning his post on common roads, at springs of water, in the shade of trees, at the foot of telegraph poles, and, lastly, quite within the defenses of the place—in the very streets of the town. A number of our men were killed by them before the disgraceful trick was discovered and information of the fact could be given to the troops. Careful examinations were at once made, and sentinels were posted wherever the existence of these infernal machines was ascertained or suspected. Major-General McClellan ordered that the Confederate prisoners taken by us at Yorktown should be made to search for these buried shells and to disinter and destroy them when found. I was myself a witness of the horrible mangling by one of these shells of a cavalryman and his horse outside of the main work upon the Williamsburg road, and also of the cruel murder in the very streets of Yorktown of an intelligent young telegraph operator, who, while in the act of approaching a telegraph pole to reconnect a broken wire, trod upon one of these shells villainously concealed at its foot. It is generally understood that these shells were prepared by General George W. Rains, of the Confederate Army, for his brother, Brig. Gen. Gabriel Rains, the commander of the post of Yorktown, at whose instigation they were prepared and planted. The belief of the complicity of General Gabriel Rains in this dastardly business is confirmed by the knowledge possessed by many officers of our Army of a similar mode of warfare inaugurated by him while disgracing the uniform of the American Army during the Seminole war in Florida.

I am, general, very respectfully, your obedient servant,

WILLIAM F. BARRY,

Brigadier-General and Inspector of Artillery, U.S. Army.

Halleck, Washington, to Lieber, New York, regarding a spy case. [WR, ser. II, vol. VI, 327–8] 30 September, 1863.

MY DEAR DOCTOR: The newspapers state that Spencer Kellogg, master's mate of Mississippi gun-boat, a prisoner of war to the rebels, was executed on Friday last. As our Government has threatened retaliation in case of such execution, if found to be unauthorized by the laws of war, it becomes necessary to examine the question with great care.

Kellogg has been held for the past year as a spy, although not captured as a spy, but as a prisoner of war. He unquestionably acted as a spy in February or March, 1862, but escaped and rejoined his ship, from which he was captured some time during the summer as an ordinary prisoner of war. We claim that not being captured while a spy, or previous to rejoining our forces, he could not be considered or treated otherwise than as a prisoner of war. This is the doctrine of paragraph 104, General Orders, No. 100. I think I have seen the same doctrine stated elsewhere, but cannot now refer to any authority. Please give me references if you have any.

I remember that the English in Major Andre's case made a point that, even admitting he was a spy, he had, when captured, passed our lines and was on "neutral grounds," and therefore no longer punishable. A ready answer to this was that lines are movable, and extend and contract with the movements of troops. Andre had not reached the British lines when captured. Had he subsequently been taken as a prisoner of war his case would have been parallel to that of Kellogg. I do not now remember a case exactly parallel. Hale was captured within the enemy's lines while acting as a spy.

The Richmond papers add that he was executed as a spy and deserter. The latter charge I think is untrue, and is probably put in as a make-weight. I saw Kellogg myself and conversed with him immediately after his return from the rebel lines, and he never intimated that he had entered the military service of the enemy.

It is important that we should take the right ground in this matter. I hope you will give me such information and advice as may be in your power.

H. W. HALLECK

M. C. Meigs, Quartermaster-General of the Union Armies, Washington, to Lieber, New York. [WR, ser. II, vol. VI, 863–4] 22 January, 1864. Meigs enquires whether enemy prisoners can be forced to work for their captors.

WASHINGTON, D. C., *January 22, 1864.*

Dr. FRANCIS LIEBER, *New York:*

DEAR SIR: In General Orders, No. 100, of 1863, section 3, paragraph 76, it is announced as a part of the law of war that prisoners of war "may be required to work for the benefit of the captors' Government, according to their rank and condition."

While at Chattanooga, where the population was thin, the army overtasked with building of bridges, roads, rebuilding railroads, and all the labors attending the repair of the communication destroyed by the rebel army, I advised the employment of some 6,000 prisoners taken in battles of Chattanooga upon public work, such as repairing the railroads which the troops from which the prisoners were captured had deliberately labored to destroy, the handling of freight, forage, rations in course of transportation to our own soldiers and to the distressed inhabitants of the country, and for the use of these very prisoners. I found the practice sanctioned by the authoritative declaration of military law of General Orders, No. 100, and had I been [in] command should have acted under it without reference to Washington for instructions. The only objections I heard urged against it at Chattanooga were the trouble of taking care of them, a trouble now only transferred to another place, and the fear of retaliation upon our men captives to the rebels. As in my own person I should much prefer labor with ax or spade or pick to rotting in idleness and sloth in prison, this had no weight with me. Labor was much needed. Warmer covering, warmer clothing, more abundant food, must be supplied these prisoners transferred to the rigorous winter climate of Chicago or Rock Island. The cost of transportation to the depot and thence to Richmond is very great. If kept near Chattanooga the time would arrive when they would be released at that place. Full fed in idleness, without exercise or mental occupation, disease will decimate them. To repair the railroads they had destroyed and to build the bridges needed in the Department of the Cumberland I have been obliged to hire in the North and East over 2,000 able-bodied men at high prices and transport them to the Department of the Cumberland, with promise of return transportation to their homes at expense of the United States. Thus expediency, efficiency, economy, and humanity appeared to me to unite in favor of the employment of these men on the public work. It was decided, however, by higher authority to be "inexpedient." I am not arguing against that decision. The prisoners have been sent North. The able-bodied mechanics and laborers to do their proper work have been hired and transmitted South. But I am convinced that, should the war continue, the policy of working prisoners of war must be finally adopted, and that public opinion will become so well instructed on this subject as to compel an advance in the true direction. The popular mind is agitated with the question of military water communication between the Atlantic and Mississippi. We feed, clothe, and shelter 40,000 rebels rotting in idleness, with no prospect of release by exchange. Why not give them a new lease of life by employing them upon this or some other such national work intended to strengthen the bonds of that Union which they have striven to destroy?

I write this for the purpose of inviting your attention to a matter which appears to me of great importance, and I would be under obligations to you for any historical precedents showing the custom or law of war on this subject in Europe. I understand that prisoners of war in France were employed by Napoleon on public work. Have not the prisoners of Mexico sent to French colonies within the past two years been so employed?

M. C. MEIGS,
Quartermaster-General.

Lieber, New York, to Meigs, Washington. [WR, ser. II, vol. VI, 868–71] 24 January, 1864.

DEAR SIR: You have treated, in your favor of the 22d, paragraph 76 of General Orders, No. 100, of 1863, so completely that I shall hardly be able to add anything of value. I recollect very well that when first the idea of giving the substance of that paragraph occurred to me I hesitated again, fearing to write down something wholly superfluous. Still, I thought of the unmeasured arrogance of our enemy—one of the motive elements of this whole war—how he pretended to lay down the most extravagant and immoral things as law for us, and I recollected an article in an Alabama journal, in which the editor called upon his authorities not to forget to send with all the troops a sufficient number of negroes to do working business, for, said he, our soldiers are all gentlemen, every one of them. I thought of all this and concluded to put down paragraph 76. It appears from your letter that I did right. Prisoners of war are universally set to work, whenever work can be found for them. If a besieged commander happens to have prisoners and is not obliged to drive them out of the fortress for want of food, it is they, before all others, who are used to repair the fortifications, to clear the streets, &c., and I have not the least hesitation in saying that a European commander who should be proved to have neglected to use prisoners for such work or for repairing bridges or railways or for fetching supplies (communication and food being quite as important as fortifications; Frederick the Great used to say: "Armies march on their bellies") would be cashiered. But the thing could never happen. Prisoners of war, however, are not only used for military work; they are set to work to do anything for which the captor can conveniently use them. The captor feeds them and clothes them and their time belongs to him. Prussian prisoners were used by Napoleon I to work on the unfinished great canals of France. Some of them used to tell me how anxious they were to be drafted for this canal work, because it gave them better food and clothing than they received in the churches or other buildings where they were huddled together and died like flies. Prussian officers frequently commanded these prisoners in the digging work. I have known officers or other educated prisoners being used for writing, &c. Of course, if they objected they could not well be forced to do such work, but then it would not have been to their advantage to do so. The liberty of the street would probably have been taken from them. I have seen French prisoners of war working as blacksmiths, &c., in making artillery or commissary wagons, &c. Perhaps a little allowance was given them; I do not know. They worked cheerfully, too. I repeat, the prisoner of war is universally put to work, if work can be found, and I think my memory does not deceive me when I say that sometimes private individuals have hired so many hundred prisoners from the Government for some great work; nay, I think the Russian Government distributed a number of French prisoners of war among the landowners, to do the work of the men who had been taken away from agriculture for the war. I speak of the war of 1810 and 1811. I think I am right, and am quite sure that it would always be done when found expedient. I recollect single French prisoners taken into service of private individuals, the Government thus getting rid of feeding them. I recollect having seen it stated in the papers that the French had used Mexican prisoners for work in their colonies. Whether this is a fact I do not know, but I do know that if they have not done so it was from no idea of delicacy or incompatibleness with the usages of war. The French are no super-refined philosophers in war. If, then, it is the universal usage of war to make prisoners work, and thus reimburse in part the expenditure they cause, the only remaining question for me in drawing up the little code was—Is there any reason of honor or humanity why this usage should be stopped? There is none whatever. The prisoner is better off for working than rotting in idleness, and if he be put to dangerous or unhealthy work, which, nevertheless, must be done, will any one say that the captor is obliged to expose his own men to the danger, rather than the enemy. I have, of course, nothing to do with the question of expediency. Expediency must be judged of in each single case on its own peculiar grounds. As a general thing, I say, as every one else will say, that it is very expedient indeed to make prisoners work and not to waste the capital that is embodied in thousands of lusty hands. I do not know whether our 50,000 prisoners are very lusty hands. The mass of Southern common people are, physically, worth very little, but work and strong food would greatly improve them.

Permit me, general, to add here that so far from my having indulged in harsh rules in the code, I have received numerous letters expressing great satisfaction at my having taken an elevated point of honor and morality. Mr. Mittermaier, one of the first jurists and publicists of the age, thanked me in very warm and flattering terms, that I had succeeded in circumscribing the military lawlessness of generals "of which we have known and suffered so much." Mittermaier is near eighty years and lives in Baden; he lived therefore on the very ground over which the overwhelming tides of the Napoleonic era flowed to and fro. I speak frankly to you, general, if I confess that I have written this whole letter in the consciousness that were an old European warrior looking over my shoulder he would smile at the idea that any one can have doubted the right and bounden duty of the captor to make use of prisoners of war. If the enemy has complained of your using prisoners to repair railways at Chattanooga, it produces on my mind an effect somewhat similar to that produced by the complaint of Soubise after his rout at Rossbach, that Frederick had attacked him at an hour so early that no French soldier could possibly have finished his hair-powder toilette. The rebel complaint, however, would be more arrogant or insolent. The French complaint was simply entertaining—a good subject for Punch. If I have left out anything which I ought to have touched upon let me know it and I will reply to the best of my ability. I have no secretary. May I beg you to keep this letter, so that, should occasion arise, I might refer to it. Or can some young epaulette make a copy of it?

I am, with great regard, your obedient servant,

FRANCIS LIEBER.

I must state to you as an inquiring officer a fact with which my correspondence arising out of code has made me acquainted, although wholly unconnected with the topic of the letter. In the wars between France and Prussia preceding that of 1813–1815 a treaty was made between the belligerents during the war that each power should pay half pay to the captured officers on its hands, the sums thus spent to be balanced in the treaty of peace whenever it should be concluded. You will allow this to be an item very remarkable in its way.

Translation.

The only canal which Bonaparte finished is that of Saint Quentin, which contains the largest known tunnel. He prosecuted other canals, commenced by his predecessors, but did not finish any of them. As to the labor of prisoners of war applied to these works my memory leaves me in doubt on the subject. After the Italian campaign in 1859 the Austrian prisoners of war sent to Africa were hired to the French colonists. I myself have made requisitions for them.

CLUSERET,
General.

P.S.—After I had finished my letter to you I received this note from General Cluseret, in our service. I made his acquaintance last night; introduced the subject of prisoners of war and the canals, the dates of which were not quite present to my mind. He promised to furnish me with the date. You will find on page 1, in the passage marked "an interesting corroboration of what I have stated," not that I approve of sending prisoners to distant colonies, or, as Russia did in 1811, to Siberia, where many French prisoners remained.

F. L.

Meigs to H. J. Raymond, editor, New York Times, *citing Lieber's authority to employ Confederate prisoners on work gangs. [WR, ser. II, vol. VI,893–4] 30 January, 1864.*

Hon. H. J. RAYMOND, *Editor of the New York Times:*

DEAR SIR: Let me invite your attention to the economic and humane considerations which affect the maintenance in idleness of our 40,000 or 50,000 prisoners of war. Employment is the law of war. See General Orders, No. 100, prepared by Doctor Lieber, and announced as to govern our armies. European nations employ them. They are made, if possible, to earn their bread. They are more healthy and more happy for the exercise. Full fed in idleness they die. We alone of all nations keep and feed and clothe 50,000 criminals as prisoners of war; enough to dig the Illinois and Michigan Ship Canal, and the Niagara Ship Canal, and establish a lasting bond of union and defense about our northern frontier in a few months' time. Only tools and powder would be needed in addition to the labor of these 50,000 idle men. Bonaparte built the canal Saint Quentin with Russian prisoners of war. Napoleon [used] the Austrian prisoners of his Italian campaign [in] Algeria, and hired them out to colonists. The subject is worth treatment in the public prints. It has not been ordered, I suppose, because the public mind has not yet been instructed and knows nothing of the laws or usages of war, but supposes that as a Christian nation we are bound to support these Southern gentlemen in idleness, well fed, til we kill them with gout or inanition. I do not wish to appear in print. I invite your attention to a subject of public importance. Let us have the value of this $50,000 a day. There is now no prospect of change, I believe.

M. C. MEIGS,
Quartermaster-General.

Meigs to Lieber. [WR, ser. II, vol. VI, 896] 1 February, 1864.

WASHINGTON, D. C., *February 1, 1864.*

Dr. FRANCIS LIEBER, *New York:*

DEAR SIR: I thank you for your letter upon the subject of employment of prisoners of war. I have spoken to some persons who will take an interest in such a matter, and do not doubt that these 50,000 pair of hands will soon be made to contribute enough at least to pay the cost of their support. I inclose a copy of your letter as requested, and am,

Very truly, your obedient servant,

M. C. MEIGS,
Quartermaster-General.

J. Holt, Judge-Advocate-General, Washington, to Stanton, Washington, [WR, ser. III, vol. IV, 1064–8] 25 January, 1865.

WAR DEPARTMENT, BUREAU OF MILITARY JUSTICE,
Washington, D. C., January 20, 1865.

Hon. E. M. STANTON,
Secretary of War:

SIR: In regard to the system of correspondence with rebels, maintained by means of an interchange of printed communications in Northern and Southern newspapers, I have the honor to present the following views in reply to the indorsement of reference of the Assistant Secretary of War of the 16th instant.

The newspapers submitted to me, as illustrating the extent to which this system is pursued, are a copy of the Richmond Inquirer, of January 10, and a copy of the New York Daily News, of January 13 last. Of the former more than five columns and a half, comprising nearly one entire side, and of the latter about three columns, or a half of one page, are taken up with the advertisements in question. These are headed "Personals," and a considerable portion of them consist of inquiries addressed from persons in the South to persons in the North, or vice versa, and of the answers thereto or to previous communications. In inserting the inquiry or notice there is generally added a request that some particular paper or papers, or that the papers generally of the opposite section, will copy it. As soon as the file is received it is copied accordingly, and if it reaches the person indicated is in due time answered by a similar insertion. A printed communication from the office of the New York Daily News, signed "by order of Benj. Wood, editor and proprietor," and transmitting one of these personals attached thereto to the party to whom it is addressed, has been referred to this Bureau, with the newspapers mentioned. From this it would seem that that journal not only prints the notice but transmits it to the address (where given) of the person for whom it is intended. It would appear from the number of the advertisements and the prices charged for their insertion that they must necessarily prove a source of considerable profit to the publishers. Upon a careful reading of these personals the following observations are suggested in regard to their character, purpose, and effect:

First. That this mode of correspondence has been resorted to in deliberate evasion and open defiance of the regulations established in regard to communication by letter between the lines. Thus, to illustrate this fact by the language employed, one of the writers remarks, "Have written several times, but as flag-of-truce mail is so irregular, prefer this mode of communication." Another says, "Have written by flag-of-truce; have received no answer; have concluded to try this channel." Another, while himself transgressing the law, unscrupulously proposed the same course to his correspondent. "As it seems," he writes, "we cannot hear from you by letter, suppose you try this medium." And in a large proportion of the notices it is expressly indicated to the party for whose eye they are intended that he should avail himself of the same form of reply.

While each of these advertisements is thus of itself a violation of the laws of war, and an evasion of the regulations referred to, it may at the same time be inferred from their terms that this evasion was in many instances of a most deliberate and criminal nature, for it is fairly to be presumed that a principal reason why former communications from the same writers had not reached their destination was because they were of an illicit or improper character, and therefore not allowed by the agent of exchange to pass the lines.

Second. That each and all of these communications is in direct violation of the regulations, in that none of them have, as is thereby required, been submitted to the inspection of the agent of exchange or his subordinate before being transmitted to their destination; that the same is to be said of a very considerable number, in that they are addressed to and signed by parties whose initials alone are given, or who are indicated by fictitious names or designations; or that they are expressed, in part at least, in language unintelligible to any one not in the confidence of the writer; or that they refer to subjects (to be presently specified) not within the limited range of those permitted by the regulations to be communicated to the enemy.

Third. That some of these advertisements treat of a class of subjects in regard to which all intercourse whatever is prohibited by the laws of war. Those principally alluded to are business transactions referring to the investment or negotiation of moneys or securities at the North for persons within the rebel lines, the transmission of money, &c., to the latter for their personal use, the receipt of money and goods, the supplying of prisoners of war with provisions and articles which under existing rules they are not permitted to receive, &c.

To illustrate this observation: A rebel in arms, a member of "Gilmor's battalion," writes from Richmond, through the New York News, to his father at the North, asking for authority to draw upon the latter for $100, as he is "very much in need of money." In another personal in the same paper a party at the North informs his correspondent at Richmond ("Theodore Thomas, care of General R. S. Ewell") that the draft of the latter for a certain amount upon a particular English house will be "honored upon presentation." One writing from the North to the South, in apparent answer to a prior communication, says: "Both draft and check are at hand, accepted, and invested as directed. Most of all the second-named are good." Another, writing from a Northern State to a correspondent, apparently a rebel, in Canada, informs him that what he "requires" will be "remitted" to him. Again, one who dates from New York addresses a female friend "near Raleigh, N. C.," asking after the "fate" of the "articles," referring, as it may well be inferred, to goods sent without authority through the lines; and one who subscribes his initials only, acknowledges the receipt from Hon. "E. M. Bruce" of a "box," for which he "cannot express his gratitude."

Not a few of the communications are from prisoners of war who in some cases apply to their relatives, &c., to be supplied not only with substantial articles of food, but with luxuries, of which they inclose extended lists, and, in other instances, they acknowledge, with expressions of satisfaction, the receipt of similar goods. It is to be observed that the rebel prisoners of war in our hands are at the present time, when our own soldiers are being systematically starved in Southern prison camps, expressly debarred, under the orders of the Commissary-General of Prisoners, from receiving any such articles as those enumerated in these advertisements, or, indeed, any articles of food not included in the daily regimen, except in cases where such may be prescribed by the surgeon of the post. To furnish them, therefore, with the provisions designated would be in direct violation of existing regulations.

Fourth. It is further to be remarked that these letters abound in expressions of personal sympathy and encouragement, which, where addressed to rebels in arms, rebel prisoners, or residents in the South, must necessarily have a very great effect in inducing them to persevere in their disloyal and traitorous purposes, assured, as they thus become, of the approbation and support of those with whom they are most nearly connected. In some of the communications the writers appeal to their correspondents at the North to administer to the wants of rebel soldiers in military custody, and in others the hopes of prisoners are excited by being informed that strenuous exertions are being used to effect their exchange. In some cases information is conveyed to parties that their friends or relatives are engaged in procuring passes to come through the lines and visit them; in others intelligence of an encouraging character is imparted in regard to the health, welfare, and circumstances of friends whom the war has separated. It is not only common soldiers and their friends who resort to these "personals" for mutual support and information, but officers also, and some of them of high rank in the rebel army, and their families, &c., make use of the same medium and for a similar purpose. It is impossible that the horrors of war should not thus be greatly alleviated for those whose crimes should justly subject them to the fullest measure of the trial and suffering which have followed upon the rebellion in which they themselves have acted a prominent part.

Fifth. It is, lastly, to be observed that a number of these advertisements are expressed in eccentric language and in terms quite incomprehensible to the general reader. These are evidently intended to convey intelligence to the parties whom they are designed to reach (but whose true names are not disclosed) which it is important to conceal from all others.

That such communications might readily be used as a cover for the transmission of material information to the public enemy is most obvious, and that they have been so employed is a legitimate presumption. Indeed, it is difficult to believe that rebel sympathizers at the North would impose such a restraint upon themselves as not to take advantage of the safe and sure medium thus opened to them for conveying aid and comfort to the cause of treason, which they delight to serve.

That the system of correspondence which has been thus examined should be forthwith put an end to by the Government would seem to admit of no question. It is a fundamental principle of public law that a declaration of war operates as an absolute interdiction of all intercourse, communication, and correspondence between the hostile powers. (1 Kent, 66; Halleck's International Law, 357.) The Executive has, indeed, adopted this principle to its utmost extent in General Orders, No. 100, of April 24, 1863, which embodies the treatise of Lieber upon the laws of war. In section 86 it is laid down as follows:

> All intercourse between the territories occupied by belligerent armies, whether by traffic, by letter, by travel, or in any other way, ceases. This is the general rule, to be observed without special proclamation. Exceptions to this rule can take place only according to agreement approved by the government or by the highest military authority. Contraventions of this rule are highly punishable.

That the Government has permitted these rules to be relaxed, and has allowed a limited correspondence to be carried on subject to certain strict regulations, can render those who abuse this privilege no less liable for a violation of the laws of war.

While there can indeed be no doubt as to the course to be pursued toward such offenders, it is to be regretted that the Government, by permitting letters from private parties to be transmitted through the lines under any circumstances or conditions, has seemed to sanction an exception to the general principle of non-intercourse and to promote the building up of the very system of correspondence through the public journals which it is now called upon to condemn and prohibit. Had the rigid rule of war interdicting all communication whatever between Southern rebels and their associates or sympathizers at the North been enforced from the beginning, and an impassable barrier thus raised between two classes of traitors who must needs depend greatly upon each other for support and encouragement, it is not unreasonable to conclude that each would have been made to feel with far more intensity and bitterness the just consequences of their atrocious treason. Moreover, shut out from all communion with those to whom they were bound by ties of kindred and friendship, they must have been far sooner discouraged in the vain but desperate struggle in which they have engaged.

On the other hand, it is to be presumed that the enemy, whether openly in arms or secretly plotting against the Government, must have been constantly infused with a new hope and courage through the medium of those facilities for intercommunication which have been afforded by our authorities.

That the interchange which has been so long pursued has at last culminated in the open, defiant, and systematic proceeding which has been commented upon serves to indicate most pointedly that for the future the disallowance altogether of the privilege of correspondence through our lines with parties in the territory of the enemy would be a most desirable measure.

But whether or not this view may approve itself to the Secretary of War, the course to be adopted for the suppression of the illicit publications which have been herein reviewed would seem to be most clear. It is recommended, therefore, that the proprietors of those newspapers in our Northern cities in which these publications have appeared be formally notified by the Government that the same must be at once wholly discontinued by them, and in case of their non-compliance with this requirement it is advised that they be brought to trial before a military commission for a violation of the laws of war.

J. HOLT,
Judge-Advocate-General.

The official orders directing Lieber as Chief of the Archives Bureau to collect and publish the archives. [WR, ser. III, vol. V, 95] 21 July, 1865.

GENERAL ORDERS, No. 127. } WAR DEPT., ADJT. GENERAL'S OFFICE, *Washington, July 21, 1865.*

Ordered, That a bureau be organized in the Adjutant-General's Office for the collection, safe-keeping, and publication of the rebel archives that have come into possession of this Government, the bureau to consist of one chief, with the pay of a colonel of cavalry, and one assistant, with the pay of a lieutenant-colonel of cavalry, and such number of clerks, to be detailed by the Adjutant-General, as may be found necessary for the speedy collection of the archives. Dr. Francis Lieber is hereby appointed chief of said bureau, and the Quartermaster-General is directed to furnish suitable apartments and buildings for the collation and custody of the archives mentioned.

By order of the Secretary of War:

E. D. TOWNSEND,
Assistant Adjutant-General.

Townsend, Washington, to Stanton, Washington. [WR, ser. II, vol. VIII, 93–4] 1 May, 1866.

SIR: In compliance with your orders I have the honor to submit copies of papers called for by resolution of the House of Representatives dated April 16, 1866, requesting "a report of the Judge-Advocate-General and such other information as may be of record or on file in his department on the subject, which will show what are the facts in the case and what steps have been taken to bring to justice and punishment the murderers of the following-named Union soldiers, belonging to the First and Second Regiments of North Carolina loyal infantry, alleged to have been tried and executed by orders of the rebel generals Pickett and Hoke, under the pretext of their being deserters from the Confederate service, viz: Jesse J. Summerlin, Hardy Dougherty, Stephen Jones, David Jones, William Haddock, John Freeman, Joseph Brock, Sergt. Joseph H. Fulcher, William D. Jones, Charles

Cuthrell, [Elijah] Kellum, Mitchell Busick, Lewis Freeman, Joseph L. Haskett, William Irving, Amos Amyett, Stephen Jones, John J. Brock."

The papers herewith are:

1. Letter of Maj. Gen. B. F. Butler to General Grant, inclosing copy of correspondence between Maj. Gen. J. J. Peck, U.S. Volunteers, and the rebel General Pickett, concerning the execution, &c., of loyal North Carolina Union soldiers.
2. Extracts from North Carolina rebel newspapers.
3. Report of a board of inquiry, and report upon the alleged murder of a large number of U.S. soldiers by the rebels during the spring of 1864, convened at New Berne, N. C., October 19, 1865.
4. Additional proceedings of same court.
5. Proceedings of second board of inquiry in case of murder of Union soldiers at Kinston, N. C., in 1864.
6. Report of Judge-Advocate-General of December 12, 1865, on memorial and other papers relating to the barbarous slaying upon the gallows of certain Union soldiers at Kinston, N. C., papers hereunto appended.
7. Report of Judge-Advocate-General of December 30, 1865, to the Secretary of War on the same subject.
8. Letter of Maj. Gen. J. J. Peck, U.S. Volunteers, of December 22, 1865, to Judge-Advocate-General.
9. Letter of Judge-Advocate-General of December 30, 1865, to Secretary of War.
10. Report of a board of inquiry convened at Raleigh, N. C., January 17, 1866, in relation to the murder of the U.S. soldiers by the rebels in March, April, and May, 1864.
11. Abstract of testimony taken before the board of inquiry convened at Raleigh, N. C., January 17, 1866, in the matter of the murder of certain U.S. soldiers at Kinston, N. C., by the rebels in 1864.
12. Letter of Maj. Gen. Thomas H. Ruger, stating that to enable him to complete the investigation ordered by the Secretary of War in relation to the murder of certain U.S. prisoners of war at Kinston, N. C., by Pickett and Hoke, he desires to be furnished

with copies of certain proceedings of the rebel court martial which tried said prisoners, with Dr. Francis Lieber's indorsement thereon stating that these proceedings are not among the records of the Archive Office.

The papers submitted show that the investigation of the transaction has been continued, under the commanding general Department of North Carolina, from the 19th October, 1865, and was progressing until the receipt of the resolution of April 16, with the view of collecting the whole testimony in proper form for such action as the President might direct.

I am, sir, very respectfully, your obedient servant,

Select Bibliography

I. Works by Lieber

Lieber, Francis. *Essays on Property and Labour as Connected with Natural Law and the Constitution of Society.* New York: Harper & Bros., 1841.

-----. *Fragments of Political Science on Nationalism and Internationalism.* New York: Chas. Scribner, 1868.

-----. *Great Events, Described by Distinguished Historians, Chroniclers and Other Writers.* New York: Harper, 1871.

-----. *Guerrilla Parties Considered with Reference to the Laws and Usages of War.* New York: D. Van Nostrand, 1862.

-----. *Legal and Political Hermeneutics or Principles of Interpretation and Construction in Law and Politics with Remarks on Precedents and Authorities.* Boston: C. C. Little & Brown, 1839.

-----. *Manual of Political Ethics.* 2 vols. Philadelphia: J. B. Lippincott, 1890.

-----. *On Civil Liberty and Self Government.* Philadelphia: J. B. Lippincott, 1859.

-----. *The Stranger in America.* 2 vols. London: R. Bentley, 1835.

II. Other Works

Brooks, L. M. "Sociology in the Works of Francis Lieber." *Social Forces* 8 (December 1929): 231–41.

Brown, Bernard Edward. *American Conservatives: The Political Thought of Francis Lieber and John W. Burgess.* New York: Columbia University Press, 1951.

Davis, G. B. "Lieber's Instructions for the Government of Armies in the Field." *American Journal of International Law* 1 (January 1907): 13–25.

Dorfman, J. "Principles of Freedom and Government Intervention in American Economic Expansion." *Journal of Economic History* 19 (December 1959): 570–83.

Friedel, Frank B., Jr. "Francis Lieber, Charles Sumner, and Slavery." *Journal of Southern History* 9 (February 1943): 75–93.

-----. "General Orders 100 and Military Government; Rules for Occupying Armies Formulated in the United States Civil War." *Mississippi Valley Historical Review* 32 (March 1946); 541–56.

-----. *Francis Lieber, Nineteenth Century Liberal.* Baton Rouge: Louisiana State University, 1947.

-----. *The Life of Francis Lieber.* Madison: University of Wisconsin Press, 1942.

Gilman, Daniel C. (ed.). *The Miscellaneous Writings of Francis Lieber.* New York: J. B. Lippincott, 1881.

Hartigan, Richard Shelly. *The Forgotten Victim: A History of the Civilian.* Chicago: Precedent, 1982.

Johnson, James Turner. *Just War Tradition and the Restraint of War.* Princeton: Princeton University Press, 1981.

Lee, Luther J., Jr. *Representative Interpretations of the Nature of the American Union: From Francis Lieber to W. W. W. Willoughby.* Berkeley: University of California Press, 1946.

Nys, Ernest. "Francis Lieber—His Life and His Work." *American Journal of International Law* 5 (January 1911): 84–117; (April 1911): 355–93.

Perry, Thomas Sergeant (ed.). *The Life and Letters of Francis Lieber.* Boston: J. R. Osgood and Co., 1882.

Phinney, Chester S. *Francis Lieber's Influence on American Thought and Some of His Unpublished Letters.* Philadelphia: University of Pennsylvania Press, 1918.

Robinson, C. B. "Francis Lieber's Nationalism." *Journal of Politics* 8 (February 1946): 57–73.

-----. "Francis Lieber's Theories of Society, Government and Liberty." *Journal of Politics* 4 (May 1942): 227–9.

Root, Elihu. "Francis Lieber and General Orders 100." *American Journal of International Law* 7 (July 1913): 453–69.

Sears, L. M. "Human Side of Francis Lieber." *South Atlantic Quarterly* 27 (January 1928): 42–61.

Wild, R. "Lieber, Korner, Schulz, drei grosse Deutsch Amerikaner." *Preuss Jahrb* 217 (July 1929): 12–27.

Woodson, C. G. "Francis Lieber, Nineteenth Century Liberal." *Journal of Negro History* 33 (July 1948): 358–61.

The following items from the Huntington Library collections have been reprinted by permission:

LI	1645–46	H. W. Halleck to F. Lieber (2 items), 1862.
LI	1649–51	H.W. Halleck to F. Lieber (3 items), 1862.
LI	1754–55	F. Lieber to H. W. Halleck (2 items), 1862.
LI	1763–66	F. Lieber to H. W. Halleck (4 items), 1862.
LI	1768–70	F. Lieber to H. W. Halleck (3 items), 1862.
LI	1778–79	F. Lieber to H. W. Halleck (2 items), 1863.
LI	1796	F. Lieber to H. W. Halleck, May 20, 1863.

Index